IMAGES
of Sport

VARSITY
CRICKET

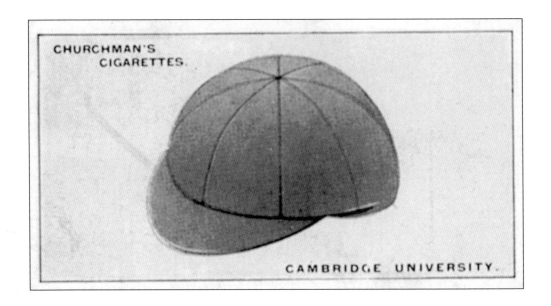

CAMBRIDGE UNIVERSITY.

OXFORD UNIVERSITY.

Above: The Cambridge University Cricket Club cap. *Below:* The Oxford University Cricket Club cap and badge.

IMAGES
of Sport

VARSITY CRICKET

Compiled by
William A. Powell

TEMPUS

First published 2001
Copyright © William A. Powell, 2001

Tempus Publishing Limited
The Mill, Brimscombe Port,
Stroud, Gloucestershire, GL5 2QG

ISBN 0 7524 1885 8

Typesetting and origination by
Tempus Publishing Limited
Printed in Great Britain by
Midway Colour Print, Wiltshire

Dedicated to all those who have represented the two Universities.

CAMBRIDGE UNIVERSITY CRICKET CLUB (J. M. Brearley)

OXFORD UNIVERSITY CRICKET CLUB (C. B. Fry)

Left: The Cambridge University light blue tie. *Right*: The Oxford University dark blue tie.

Contents

Preface

The 2001 season will see a one-day match at Lord's Cricket Ground for the first time on 28 June, plus the annual Varsity Match between the two famous premier University Cricket sides to be staged between Cambridge and Oxford at Fenner's, Cambridge between 30 June and 3 July.

As all cricketers and spectators are aware, the first few days of each new cricket season in an English spring commence with early fixtures between the Universities and the counties. These are staged at the delightful tree-lined University Parks in Oxford and the attractive and welcoming University Cricket Ground at Fenner's in Cambridge, situated only a short walk from Parker's Piece and the city centre of Cambridge.

This collection of old archive photographs and items of cricket interest are sure to please those who played for either of the great Universities or witnessed matches at the Parks, Fenner's or Lord's over the last century. The various photographs will give readers a good view of the teams and faces that played University Cricket from the 1870s to the end of the last century. Included are a number of the names behind the great University teams such as Pelham Warner, Peter May, Raman Subba Row, Doug Insole, Colin Cowdrey, Tony Lewis, Mike Brearley, Imran Khan and Mike Atherton, all of whom represented the light and dark blues with distinction.

The author would like to thank the following who have assisted in a variety of ways in the preparation of this book, including the following who kindly loaned me some photographic material for inclusion in the book from their archive photograph collections:
Dennis Silk OBE, Tim Lamb, Alan C. Smith CBE, Donald B. Carr OBE, Tony Pawson OBE, Peter W.G. Powell, Dr Simon Porter, the late Jack Davies, Mark Nicholls, Mike Brearley OBE, Raman Subba Row CBE, Hubert Doggart, the late Lord Cowdrey of Tonbridge CBE, Tony Lewis, Mike Tarr, the late E.W. 'Jim' Swanton, Deryck Murray, Doug Insole CBE, Vic Lewis, Brian Croudy, Kate Wiseman, Rosie Knowles and James Howarth.

I acknowledge the sources of the illustrations, which are many and include the Cambridge University and Oxford University Cricket Clubs, A. Henry, Hills & Saunders, Stearn, Kay Chadwick, Gillman & Co., Daily Graphic, Elliott & Fry and my own collection of picture postcards, cigarette cards and scorecards, magazines and newspapers. Apologies are offered to anyone whose photographs have inadvertently been used without acknowledgement.

William A. Powell
Hemel Hempstead, Hertfordshire
March 2001

Bibliography

A History of the Cambridge University Cricket Club 1820-1901 by W.J. Ford (William Blackwood & Sons) 1901, History of the O.U.C.C. by Geoffrey Bolton (The Holywell Press Ltd) 1962, MCC Scores & Biographies Vol. 1 to 14, Fifty Years of Sport at Oxford, Cambridge and the Great Public Schools, Fifty Years of Sport at the Universities, Oxford Memories and The Cricket Field by Rev. J. Pycroft, Famous Cricketers and Cricket Grounds by C.W. Alcock 1895, The Book of Cricket by C.B. Fry 1895, Oxford versus Cambridge by H.M. Abrahams and J. Bruce-Kerr 1931, The Jubilee Book of Cricket by K.S. Ranjitsinhji, The Badminton Book of Cricket, The Elevens of the Three Great Public Schools, Records of the Harlequin Cricket Club 1857-1926 by A.J.H. Cochrane, Sporting Pie by F.B. Wilson, Cambridge University Cricketers 1820-1992 by P.Thorn and P.J. Bailey.

Fenner's University Cricket Ground, Cambridge in 1993.

Introduction (Cambridge)

There have been few moments in my life that have given me a greater thrill than the moment at which my captain, Robin Marlar, invited me to play against Oxford at Lord's in the Varsity match. The nervous tension that had built up in my mind had made batting at Fenner's against professional county bowlers a more traumatic experience than any I had met before on a sports field. Against Middlesex, at a crucial moment, I had to weather a torrid half hour against the bowling of John Warr and Don Bennett at the end of a testing day in the field. I vividly remember playing and missing at a whole over from Bennett and was not greatly comforted at the end of the over by a polite enquiry from the Middlesex wicketkeeper, Leslie Compton. With a slow smile he asked me: 'Have you ever tried walking on water?'

The thought of wearing the powder blue cap and blazer was a thought that had become a regular part of my dreams. The void that separates club cricket from first-class cricket is a huge one, and so far as cricket is concerned the only bigger void, I imagine, is that which separates first-class cricket from Test cricket. The whole process of winning a blue is one that is apt to become grotesquely out of proportion to the aspirant and a mystery to those who have no particular interest in sport. To say to a Cambridge man who is going to Lord's to play Oxford; 'Don't worry, it's only a game', would be regarded as a bad joke. It is most salutory to those involved in a Varsity match to realise that the match which has become an obsession to them is regarded almost as an irrelevance by the great English public.

The focus on one all-important match may seem unbalanced and a negation of true sport, but there is no doubt at all that it adds spice and a pressure which has all the intensity of a Test Match. It is a real test of nerve, as well as of skill. Many fine internationals have failed in Varsity matches, while several very ordinary players have enjoyed moments of triumph. Cobden, whose legendary hat-trick at the climax of an extraordinary Varsity match has become a part of the folklore of English cricket, was never thought of as an England player. Peter May, on the other hand, was England's greatest post-war batsman and he never made a fifty in three matches. John Pretlove, who would never have considered himself as being even a distant rival of Peter May as a batsman, never looked like failing in a Varsity match, and that also applied in his soccer (of which he was captain) and rugby fives, in which he was national champion – he was a great natural all-round athlete with a perfect temperament for big occasions.

Looking back now over nearly fifty years to the roseate haze of undergraduate cricket at Fenner's and on tour, one has little difficulty in seeing what really matters most. The friendships forged in playing cricket for Cambridge and Oxford were what matter most. The University sides have unlimited scope for developing team spirit and tactical awareness. For most of those competing for places in the team it quickly dawns that this game is the subtlest of all team games. Playing six days a week for eight weeks, as was formerly the custom, against seasoned professionals who were anxious to help and advise over a pint or two of beer at the end of the day was a privilege indeed. By degrees the fielders began to work as one, eyes constantly on the captain for the slightest signal, knowing how many balls had been bowled in the over so that a batsman could be kept at one end if that was required. In batting, the same awareness was built up. Mid-on might seem ponderous in the field and there was a single to him if both of you were alert for it. Cover-point was left-handed. The new batsman coming in was on a pair and needed help in getting off the mark. We also learned to rejoice with our rivals for a place in the side when they did well and we did badly. Under a selfless, inspirational captain like Mike Bushby, we were a thoroughly happy and purposeful unit and most of us are still in touch today.

Many fine England players graduated to international cricket through Fenner's and the Parks. I arrived in Cambridge in a year in which the University could call on five Test players: David Sheppard, Peter May, Cuan McCarthy, Raman Subba Row and Gerry Alexander. Before them had gone John Dewes, Hubert Goggart and Doug Insole. It was a golden age indeed, but when one looked even further back to Freddie Brown, Billy Griffith, Ken Farnes, the Ashton brothers, Percy Chapman, Gubby Allen and a host of others almost equally distinguished, one realises how much the products of University cricket have put back into the game. Some became presidents of the MCC, even more sat on the MCC Committee. Cricket had been good to them and they regarded themselves as custodians of the values and friendships the game had given them.

No wonder, then, that Cyril Coote, the devoted, shrewd old groundsman at Fenner's, should have so delighted to tell us, when we were fresh-faced undergraduates, stories of heroic events on his cricket ground in times past. We were being admitted to a fellowship of men who were far greater than any of us, who had worn the pale blue cap, cared deeply about Cambridge cricket and helped to make English cricket revered in every corner of the world. What a pity it would be if such tradition were to be broken. Those who hold the key to the future are the Tutors for Admission who appear to believe that brilliance on the sports field and academic excellence are mutually exclusive. I hope they wake up in time.

Dennis Silk.

D.R.W. Silk OBE
Cambridge University, Somerset and MCC
March 2001

The Pavilion at University Parks Cricket Ground, Oxford in 1992.

Introduction (Oxford)

As a youngster my favourite reading was the cricket section of the great tome covering fifty years of Oxbridge sport. Since then there have been two histories of the OUCC, but I have not seen one devoted to both Universities. So I was delighted to know it is the latest subject of William Powell's book in the *Images of Sport* series.

I was sure the OUCC books would celebrate adequately the family record of my father, Guy, and I each captaining Oxford to an innings victory. Of the 1910 match, one recorded that Oxford won despite the extraordinary captaincy of A.G. Pawson, while the other concentrated on my failure to select Donald Carr. Still you can't do much better than win by an innings, particularly when Cambridge fielded four future Test Players (Trevor Bailey, Doug Insole, Hubert Doggart and John Dewes) against our two (Abdul Hafeez Kardar and Clive van Ryneveld).

As that was fifty-one years ago, it must qualify as antique archive material. But my uncle Clive was on the winning Oxford side in 1901 and my father, Guy, helped Oxford to three wins and a favourable draw from 1908 to 1911. So Father seems best suited for archive memories.

He used to tell how the game in his day was more sporting. Two Varsity match incidents made me wonder. Keeping to the bowling of Gilbert, who ran through the Australians so quickly at Oxford that he was made twelfth man for the next Test, Father saw the Cambridge opener, Young, snick the ball into his pads.

Sublimely ignorant of the laws, he assumed Young would be out if he scooped the ball out. As he delved with his glove, Young defended himself vigorously. Battered, but triumphant, father emerged with the ball. The whole Oxford team appealed only to be rebuked by the umpire and criticised by *The Times*.

His year of captaincy (1910) became know as 'Le Couteur's match'. The Australian came in with three early wickets lost and rattled up 160 runs. He ran through the Cambridge batting twice with his leg-spinners. That was the best all-round performance ever in these matches.

Le Couteur was dropped three times by an unfortunate man. He had been the last awarded his blue, partly due to his excellent fielding. The experience so shattered him that coming to bat in a daze, he tried to take guard facing Father. With exemplary sportsmanship, Father turned him round and pointed out the umpire. It was just bad luck (so he maintained) that he left him a few inches outside his crease, and recorded another stumping when he made no attempt to play his first ball.

Father is probably the only man not to know he was on a winning side until a month later. Even keener on fishing than cricket, he had to be persuaded by his elder brother to accept his freshman blue, despite the Varsity match interfering with a planned holiday in Scotland. A storm appeared to have left further play impossible, with Oxford needing 38 to win with three wickets left. Already out, Father hurried off to catch the train north. Only on his return did he find that the pitch had been mopped up and the injured Teesdale, batting one-handed, had steered Oxford home.

Douglas Jardine was a notorious Oxford captain. A demon to some, he was my schoolboy hero. Winning 4-1 in Australia was a rare Ashes celebration in my youth, and at Horris Hill, Jardine's prep school, we were given a whole day's holiday. Magic! Jardine designed 'fast leg theory' to combat the invincible Don Bradman who still averaged over fifty. A whinging Aussie then christened it 'bodyline' and the rumpus started.

In fact, it was mild stuff compared to Lillee and Thomson later, or some West Indian fast bowlers, but our shaken authorities soon abandoned Jardine, Larwood and Voce and returned to being good losers. Jardine followed Cambridge's 'Percy' Chapman as England captain, one of only two to share a remarkable treble of centuries at Lord's (in the Varsity match, for the Gentlemen, and in a Test).

The other, Martin Donnelly, was my inspirational captain in my debut year. New Zealand's greatest batsman scored 142 for Oxford, 162 for the Gents, and 206 against England. On that tour New Zealand played thirty-two matches, including Tests, and lost only once … to Oxford, of course.

When Donnelly received a note of congratulation from Chapman, it ended with the traditional greeting G.D.B.O., short for God damn bloody Oxford. But having had a son at Cambridge (because of its superior science, rather than cricket) and joined their footballers in Pegasus's Cup winning runs, I appreciate the quality of their cricket and many other sports.

Tony Pawson

H.A. Pawson OBE
Oxford University, Kent and MCC
March 2001

One

The Beginnings

Charles Wordsworth (Harrow and Christ Church, Oxford), represented Oxford University in 1827 and 1829 and he captained the side during that period. In 1827 the Varsity fixture was drawn at Lord's but two years later, in 1829, Wordsworth led Oxford to victory by 115 runs. Match details were Oxford 129 and 158, with Cambridge replying with 96 and 76.

Born in Mayfair, London in 1809, The Hon. Robert Grimston (Harrow and Christ Church, Oxford) in 1845 succeeded as 2nd Earl of Verulam near St. Albans in Hertfordshire and represented Oxford University between 1828 and 1830. Schooled at Harrow, he only played one match whilst at Oxford and his final first-class match was for the Married versus the Singles in 1849. He had previously played for the Gentlemen between 1836 and 1839, MCC between 1830 and 1843 and Hertfordshire in 1835. He was MCC President in 1867 and was MP for St Albans in 1830/31 and Hertfordshire between 1832 and 1845. He died at Gorhambury House, near St Albans in 1895.

Cambridge University students playing cricket at Parker's Piece in 1842.

Sir H. Meredyth Plowden (Harrow and Trinity, Cambridge) was born in Sylhet, India in 1840. He represented Cambridge University between 1860 and 1863, attaining blues in all four years, and he captained the light blues between 1862 and 1863. A stylish middle order batsman and right-arm off-break bowler, he later went on to play for Hampshire in a single match in 1865. Also a good rackets player, his first-class cricket career was rather short, as he moved to India in 1877, where he remained until 1894 as Judge of the Chief Court in the Punjab. His last first-class match was in 1866 for MCC. In total, Plowden played 15 matches scoring 248 runs (av. 13.05) with a highest innings of 69 not out. He bagged 56 wickets (av. 12.83) with a best performance of 7 for 25 and he held 10 catches. He died in 1920 in Sunninghill, Berkshire.

Part of the Cambridge University XI of 1861. From left to right, standing: (Sir) H.M. Plowden, The Hon. C.G. Lyttelton (Viscount Cobham). Seated: T.E. Bagge (captain), H.M. Marshall.

Born at Southgate, Middlesex in 1842, Russell Walker (Harrow and Brasenose, Oxford), brother of Alfred (Middlesex), A.H. (Middlesex), Frederic (Middlesex), John (Middlesex), Isaac D. (Middlesex) and Vyell E. (Middlesex), and nephew of Henry (MCC 1832), was a right-handed, attacking opening batsman, right-hand slow round-arm bowler and good fielder. He attended Harrow School and then went on to Oxford University, where he attained blues all five years between 1861 and 1865. He represented Middlesex 45 times between 1862 and 1877, during which time he amassed 1,678 runs (av. 22.07). He scored a single century of 104 and he bagged 142 wickets (av. 17.54) with a best performance of 6 for 76. His best season was 1865, when he recorded 770 runs (av. 24.83) and his last first-class match was for MCC in 1878. He was a committee member of both MCC and Middlesex until his death, having served as president of Middlesex CCC from 1906 to 1922 and as a trustee of MCC. He represented Oxford University at rackets, being a notable player. He died at Regent's Park, London in 1922.

Oxford University XI in 1863, who defeated Cambridge in the Varsity Match by 8 wickets. From left to right, back row: S.C. Voules, J. Scott, H.E. Bull, F.R. Evans, R.A.H. Mitchell (captain), E.T. Daubeney, T.P. Garnier, A.S. Teape, F.G. Inge. Front row: F.W. Wright, J.W. Haygarth and R.D. Walker. At Lord's on 22 and 23 June, Cambridge scored 65 and 61, Oxford replied with 59 and 68 for 2.

Cambridge University XI in 1863. From left to right, back row: H.M. Marshall, F.C. Hope-Grant, T. Collins, Hon. T. de Grey, Hon. C.G. Lyttelton, C. Booth, A.W.T. Daniel. Front row: G.H. Tuck, H.M. Plowden (captain), G.F. Helm, R.D. Balfour.

Survivors of the Cambridge University XI in 1863, on 8 July 1908. From left to right, back row: H.M. Marshall, T. Collins, The Hon. T. de Grey (Lord Walsingham), The Hon. C.G. Lyttelton (Viscount Cobham), C. Booth. Front row: G.H. Tuck, (Sir) H.M. Plowden (captain), R.D. Balfour.

1866.

Oxford University XI in 1866 who defeated Cambridge in the Varsity Match at Lord's by the narrow margin of 12 runs. From left to right, top row: E.S. Carter, E.W. Titton (captain), E.M. Kenney. Second row: G.P. Robertson, W.F. Maitland, C.E. Boyle. Third row: E.L. Fellows, R.T. Reid, E. Davenport. Bottom row: S.C. Voules, O. Spencer-Smith. Oxford scored 62 and 171, with Cambridge recording 128 and 93. E.L. Fellowes recorded match figures of 13 for 88.

Oxford University XI in 1868. From left to right, from top to bottom:
E.L. Fellowes (captain),
A.C. Batholomew, E.M. Kenney,
E. Mathews, B. Pauncefote,
A.T. Fortescue, W.H. Lipscomb,
R. Didby, R.F. Miles, R.T. Reid,
W. Evetts. Cambridge beat Oxford in the Varsity Match at Lord's on 22, 23 and 24 June by 168 runs. The match details were Cambridge 111 and 236 with Oxford replying with 88 and 91.

1868

Oxford University XI in 1869. From left to right, from top to bottom: B. Pauncefote (captain), A.F. Walker, R.F. Miles, F.H. Hill, E.F.S. Tylecote, W.A. Stewart, J.H. Gibbon, W. Evetts, A.T. Fortescue, R. Digby, E. Mathews. Cambridge beat Oxford by 58 runs in the Varsity Match at Lord's on 21 and 22 June. Cambridge made 164 and 91, Oxford 99 and 98, with W.B. Money recording match figures of 11 for 59.

1869.

Cuthbert John Ottaway (Eton and Brasenose, Oxford), was born in Dover, Kent in 1850. He represented Oxford University between 1870 and 1873 and he captained the side in the last of his three years at University. A sound middle order batsman and wicketkeeper, he later played for Kent (1869-70 in 2 matches) and Middlesex (1874-76 in 7 matches) before he retired on being called to the Bar. In 1872 he toured North America with R.A. Fitzgerald's team. Ottaway was without doubt the best amateur batsman of his day and he was an outstanding sportsman, also representing the dark blues at athletics, rackets, royal tennis and association football, and appearing twice at international level for England. In total he played 37 first-class matches, scoring 1,691 runs (av. 27.27) with a top score of 112. He held 22 catches and achieved a single stumping. He died in Westminster, London in 1878.

17

Cambridge University XI in 1870. From left to right, top row: F.C. Cobden, E.E.H. Ward, C.I. Thornton, W. Yardley. Middle row: F.A. Mackinnon, W.B. Money (captain), F. Tobin. Front row: A.A. Bourne, A.T. Scott, F.E.R. Fryer, J.W. Dale. Cambridge beat Oxford by 2 runs at Lord's on 27 and 28 June. It was known as 'Cobden's match' because of F.C. Cobden, who won the match for Cambridge in the last over of the game. Cambridge recorded 147 and 206 (W. Yardley 100) with Oxford scoring 175 and 176 in reply.

Oxford University XI in 1870. From left to right, top row: C.K. Francis, C.J. Ottaway, E.F.S. Tylecote, A.T. Fortescue. Middle row: W. Townshend, B. Pauncefote (captain), W.H. Hadow. Bottom row: F.H. Hill, T.H. Belcher, S.E. Butler, W.A. Stewart.

Oxford University XI in 1871. From left to right, top row: W. Law, E.F.S. Tylecote (captain), S.E. Butler, Hon. G.F.R. Harris. Middle row: B. Pauncefote, W. Townshend, C.K. Francis. Front row: C. Marriott, C.J. Ottaway, W.H. Hadow, S. Pelham. Oxford won the Varsity Match by 8 wickets when Cambridge was defeated at Lord's on 26 and 27 June. Match details were Oxford 170 and 25 for 2, with Cambridge scoring 65 and 129 in response.

Born in Trinidad in 1851, when his father was Governor, Lord Harris – formerly The Hon. G.R.C. Harris (Eton and Christ Church, Oxford) – captained Eton to victory versus Harrow at Lord's in 1870. Later that season he began his sixty year association with Kent, making his debut versus MCC at Canterbury. Whilst at Oxford University he attained four blues between 1871 and 1874 and during 1872 he toured Canada with R.A. Fitzgerald's team. In 1875 he was appointed Kent CCC president, captain and secretary. He took a side to Australia in 1878/79 when he took it upon himself to end the Anglo-Australian cricket crisis. In 1882 he made his highest score of 176 for Kent versus Sussex at Gravesend. Playing 157 matches for Kent he scored 7,842 runs (av. 30.04) with 10 centuries, took 64 wickets (av. 23.79) and he held 155 catches. Later, as the Governor of Bombay, he organised the first English tour to India and he fought in the Boer War. Playing four Tests, he was the oldest man to play first-class cricket at 60 years 151 days for Kent versus All India at Catford in 1911.

Cambridge University XI in 1871. Left to right, top row: F.C. Cobden, E.E.H. Ward, C.I. Thornton, F. Tobin. Middle row: W.N. Powys, W.B. Money, W. Yardley (captain). Front row: E. Bray, A.T. Scott, F.E.R. Fryer, H.C.P. Stedman.

Cambridge University XI in 1872, who beat Oxford in the Varsity Match at Lord's on 24 and 25 June by an innings and 166 runs. From left to right, top row: G.S. Raynor, E. Bray, E.P. Baily, F.E.R. Fryer. Middle row: F.C. Cobden, F. Tobin, W. Yardley. Front row: G.H. Longman, C.I. Thornton (captain), W.N. Powys, A.S. Tabor. Match details were: Cambridge 388 (W. Yardley 130), Oxford 72 and 150 with W.N. Powys recording match figures of 13 for 65.

Oxford University XI in 1872. From left to right, top row: C.J. Ottaway, W. Law, S.E. Butler, W.H. Hadow. Middle row: A.W. Ridley, E.F.S. Tylecote (captain), Hon. G.F.R. Harris. Front row: F.W. Isherwood, C.A. Wallroth, C.K. Francis, W. Townshend.

Oxford University XI in 1873. From left to right, top row: W.H. Game, W. Law, C.J. Ottaway (captain), and E.S. Garnier. Middle row: C.A. Wallroth, S.E. Butler, C.W. Boyle, C.K. Francis. Front row: C.E.B. Nepean (Lord Harris), A.W. Ridley, J. Maude. Oxford won the Varsity Match by 3 wickets. Cambridge were 152 and 203, Oxford were 182 and 177 for 7.

Cambridge University XI in 1873. From left to right, top row: G.E. Jeffrey, H.A. Douglas-Hamilton, H.M. Sims, A.S. Tabor. Middle row: T. Latham, F.E.R. Fryer (captain), C. Tillard. Front row: W. Blacker, G.H. Longman, G.H. Hone-Goldney, W.J. Ford. During the Varsity Match of 1873, G.E. Jeffery achieved bowling figures of 8 for 44 in an innings.

Oxford University XI in 1874, who defeated Cambridge in the Varsity Match at Lord's on 29 and 30 June by an innings and 92 runs. From left to right, top row: W.H. Game, C.A. Wallroth, Lord Harris, D. Campbell. Middle row: W. Foord-Kelcey, W. Law (captain), A.W. Ridley. Front row: W.W. Pulman, T.W. Lang, H.G. Tylecote, T.B. Jones. Cambridge recorded 109 and 65, and T.W. Lang recorded match figures of 10 for 74, with Oxford scoring 265.

Cambridge University XI in 1874.
From left to right, top row: T. Latham,
C. Tillard, H.M. Sims, G.E. Jeffery.
Middle row: F.F.J. Greenfield, G.H.
Longman (captain), A.S. Tabor. Front
row: E.P. Baily, G. Macan,
W.N. Powys, W. Blacker.

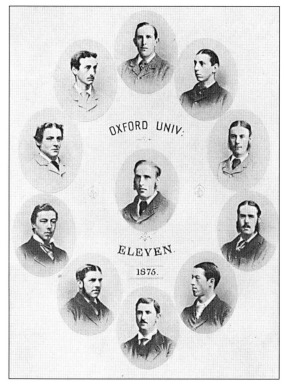

Oxford University XI in 1875 who
defeated Cambridge in the Varsity
Match by 6 runs at Lord's on
28, 29 and 30 June. From left to right,
top row: T.W. Lang, A.W. Ridley
(captain), R. Briggs. Middle row:
A.J. Webbe, W.W. Pulman, W. Foord-
Kelcey. Front row: W.H. Game,
V.P.F.A. Royle, D. Campbell,
H.G. Tylecote, F.M. Buckland. Details
of the match were: Oxford 200 and
137, with Cambridge responding with
163 and 168.

Born in Bethnal Green, London in 1855, brother of H.R. (Middlesex) and G.A. (MCC), Alexander Webbe (Harrow and Trinity, Oxford), was a stylish right-handed opening batsman, right-arm fast medium bowler, specialist mid-wicket fielder and occasional wicketkeeper. Schooled at Harrow, he went on to Oxford University, attaining blues in all four years between 1875 and 1878 and captaining the side in 1877 and 1878. He represented Middlesex 247 times between 1875 and 1900. During his career he scored 14,465 runs (av. 24.81) with 14 centuries including a top score of 243 not out for Middlesex versus Yorkshire at Huddersfield in 1897. He bagged 109 wickets (av. 25.21) with a best haul of 5 for 23, and he held 228 catches and took 10 stumpings. His best county season was 1887, when he recorded 1,244 runs (av. 47.84). He captained Middlesex between 1885 and 1898, being joint leader with Andrew Stoddart in 1898. He acted as Middlesex CCC secretary between 1900 and 1922 and was club president during the period 1923 to 1936. A useful rackets player and footballer, he represented Oxford University in both sports. He died at Fulvens, Hoe, Abinger Hammer, Surrey in 1941.

Born in Westminster, London in 1857, Alfred Lucas (Uppingham and Clare, Cambridge), cousin of C.F. (Hampshire), was a right-handed opening batsman, slow round-arm bowler and fine fielder. Lucas achieved blues all four years whilst at Cambridge between 1875 and 1878. He played 28 matches for Cambridge, scoring 1,287 runs (av. 32.17) with a top score of 105. He bagged 20 wickets (av. 16.40) with a best haul of 5 for 34 and he held 19 catches. Lucas played later for Surrey, Middlesex and Essex in a total of 256 matches during his career, accumulating 10,263 runs (av. 26.38) with a top score of 145. He bagged 155 wickets (av. 18.38) with a best performance of 6 for 10, and he held 152 catches. He also represented England in five Tests between 1878/79 to 1884 and he went on tour to Australia in 1878/79. He died at Great Waltham, Essex in 1923.

Cambridge University XI in 1875.
From left to right, top row: G. Macan,
W. Blacker, H.A. Douglas-Hamilton,
H.M. Sims. Middle row:
F.F.J. Greenfield, C.H. Longman
(captain), Hon. E. Lyttelton. Front
row: A.P. Lucas, A.F. Smith,
C.M. Sharpe, W.S. Patterson.

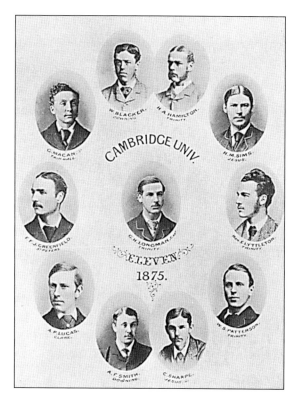

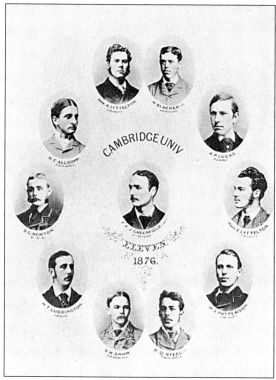

Cambridge University XI in 1876.
From left to right, top row:
H.T. Allsopp, Hon. A. Lyttelton,
W. Blacker, A.P. Lucas. Middle row:
S.C. Newton, F.F.J. Greenfield
(captain), Hon. E. Lyttelton. Front
row: H.T. Luddington, V.K. Shaw,
D.Q. Steel, W.S. Patterson. Cambridge
beat Oxford by 9 wickets in the Varsity
Match at Lord's on 26, 27 and 28 June.
Oxford had 112 and 262 (W.H. Game
109), Cambridge 302 (W.S. Patterson
105 not out) and 76 for 1.

Oxford University XI in 1876. From left to right, top row: C.P. Lewis, A.H. Heath, F.M. Buckland, H.G. Tylecote. Middle row: V.P.F.A. Royle, W.H. Game (captain), A. Pearson. Front row: A.J. Webbe, R. Briggs, T.S. Dury, D. Campbell.

Oxford University XI in 1877. From left to right, top row: A.D. Greene, F.M. Buckland, H.G. Tylecote, E.W. Wallington. Middle row: A.H. Heath, A.J. Webbe (captain), F.C.E. Jellicoe. Front row: A. Pearson, J.H. Savory, H.R. Webbe, H. Fowler. Oxford defeated Cambridge by 10 wickets at Lord's on 25 and 26 June in the Varsity Match. Cambridge recorded 134 and 126. Oxford replied with 214 (F.M. Buckland 117 not out) and 47 for 0. Oxford achieved their lowest innings total ever of just 12 against MCC at the University Parks in 1877.

Fenner's Old Cricket Pavilion, Cambridge that was removed in approximately 1877.

Cambridge University XI in 1877. From left to right, top row:
H.T. Luddington, S.S. Schultz, L. Bury, F.H. Mellor. Middle row:
A.P. Lucas, W.S. Patterson (captain), Hon. E. Lyttelton. Front row:
Hon. A. Lyttelton, L.K. Jarvis, H. Pigg, D.Q. Steel.

Cambridge University XI in 1878. From left to right, back row: Hon. I.F.W. Bligh, D.Q. Steel, L.K. Jarvis, A.F.J. Ford. Middle row: F.W. Kingston, A.P. Lucas, Hon. E. Lyttelton (captain), Hon. A. Lyttelton, P.H. Morton. Front row: H. Whitfield, A.G. Steel. Cambridge beat Oxford by the mammoth margin of 238 runs in the Varsity Match at Lord's on 1 and 2 July. Cambridge made 168 and 229, Oxford 127 and 32, A.G. Steel recording match figures of 13 for 73.

Born at Westminster in 1859, the Hon. Ivo Bligh (Eton and Trinity, Cambridge) who became the 8th Earl of Darnley in 1900, was a tall, stylish batsman and a fine fielder. He made his first-class debut for Kent in 1877, scoring a total of 1,493 runs (av.18.89) with a top score of 105. He later played for Cambridge University between 1878 and 1881 (captaining the light blues in 1881), when he gained a blue as a freshman and represented the University when they beat the touring Australians in 1878 by an innings. He led the first England team that recovered 'The Ashes' in 1882/83, after they had been created by a mock obituary following the defeat at Kennington Oval in August 1882. His England side of 1882/83 became the first team to play Ceylon when their ship docked at Colombo en-route to Australia. He played all four of his Tests in Australia, scoring 62 runs (av. 10.33) with a top score of 19 at Sydney and holding 7 catches. He represented the Cambridge Crusaders CC whilst at University. After his death in 1927, his widow presented 'The Ashes' urn to the MCC Museum.

Oxford University XI in 1878. From left to right, back row: H.R. Webbe, J.H. Savory, A.H. Heath, G.S. Marriott, C.W.M. Kemp. Front row: A.D. Greene, R.L. Knight, A.P. Wickham, A.J. Webbe (captain), A.H. Evans, E.T. Hirst. Oxford University scored 32 against Cambridge University during the Varsity Match at Lord's, which was the lowest innings total recorded against Cambridge in University match history.

Born in West Derby, Liverpool in 1858, Allan Steel was an attacking right-handed batsman and a slow/medium bowler. Steel (Marlborough, Trinity Hall, Cambridge), represented Cambridge University between 1878 and 1881 and he captained the side in 1880, attaining blues in all four years. He later represented Lancashire between 1877 and 1893 in 47 matches and toured Australia with Ivo Bligh in 1882/83. He made his Test debut in 1880 and played thirteen times for England, until 1888. President of MCC in 1902, he also won blues for rackets whilst at University. In total he played 162 matches scoring exactly 7,000 runs (av. 29.41) with a top score of 171. He bagged 789 wickets (av. 14.78), with a best haul of 9 for 63 for Lancashire against Yorkshire at Old Trafford, Manchester in 1878. He died in Hyde Park, London in 1914.

Oxford University XI in 1879. From left to right, top row: A.H. Heath, A.D. Greene, A.H. Evans, A. Haskett-Smith. Middle row: E.T. Hirst, H.R. Webbe (captain), H. Fowler. Front row: F.G.G. Jellicoe, W.A. Thornton, N. MacLachlan, J.H.M. Hare.

Cambridge University XI in 1879. From left to right, top row: P.H. Morton, H. Wood, R.S. Jones, L.K. Jarvis. Middle row: H. Whitfield, Hon. A. Lyttelton (captain), G.B. Studd. Front row: A.F.J. Ford, D.Q. Steel, A.G. Steel, Hon. I.F.W. Bligh. Cambridge won the Varsity Match by the margin of 9 wickets thanks to A.G. Steel, who recorded match figures of 11 for 66. Oxford totalled 149 and 64 with Cambridge replying with 198 and 16 for 1.

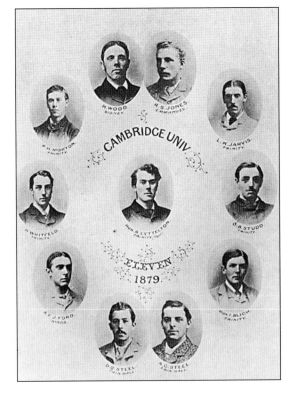

Two

Early Years

Charles Studd (Eton and Trinity, Cambridge) was born in 1860 in Spratton, Northamptonshire. He represented Cambridge University between 1880 and 1883 and he captained the light blues in 1883, his last season at Fenner's. Whilst at Cambridge he played 31 matches and scored 1,852 runs (av. 39.40) with a highest score of 175 not out, bagged 130 wickets (av. 16.30) with a best haul of 8 for 40 and he held 24 catches. He later also represented Middlesex, between 1879 and 1884 in 34 matches, the Gentlemen of India in 1902/03 and England in five Tests between 1882 and 1882/83. He died in Ibambi, Belgian Congo in 1931.

Cambridge University XI in 1880. From left to right, top row: C.P. Wilson, C.W. Foley, O.P. Lancashire, R.S. Jones. Middle row: A.F.J. Ford, A.G. Steel (captain), Hon. I.F.W. Bligh. Front row: H. Whitfield, G.B. Studd, C.T. Studd, P.H. Morton. Cambridge won the Varsity Match staged at Lord's on 28 and 29 June by 115 runs. Cambridge scored 166 and 232, Oxford 132 and 151, with A.G. Steel recording match figures of 10 for 98.

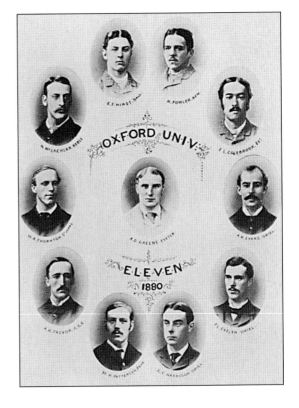

Oxford University XI in 1880. From left to right, top row: N. MacLachlan, E.T. Hirst, H. Fowler, E.L. Colebrook. Middle row: W.A. Thornton, A.D. Greene (captain), A.H. Evans. Front row: A.H. Trevor, W.H. Patterson, G.C. Harrison, F.L. Evelyn.

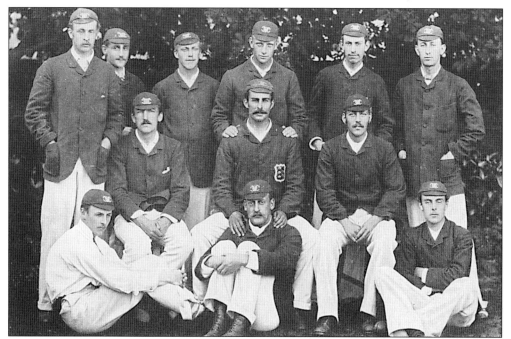

Oxford University XI in 1881. From left to right, back row: E. Peake, A.O. Whiting, W.A. Thornton, C.F.H. Leslie, M.C. Kemp, G.E. Robinson. Middle row: A.H. Trevor, A.H. Evans (Captain), W.H. Patterson. Front row: W.H. Heale, N. MacLachlan, G.C. Harrison. Oxford beat Cambridge at Lord's in the Varsity Match by 135 runs. Oxford made 131 and 306 (W.H. Patterson 107 not out), Cambridge 179 and 123. A.H. Evans recorded match bowling figures of 13 for 130 for the dark blues.

Cambridge University XI in 1881. From left to right, back row: C.T. Studd, H. Whitfield, J.E.K. Studd, F.C.C. Rowe, C.P. Wilson. Front row: N. Hone, G.B. Studd, Hon. I.F.W. Bligh (Captain), A.G. Steel, A.F.J. Ford, R. Spencer.

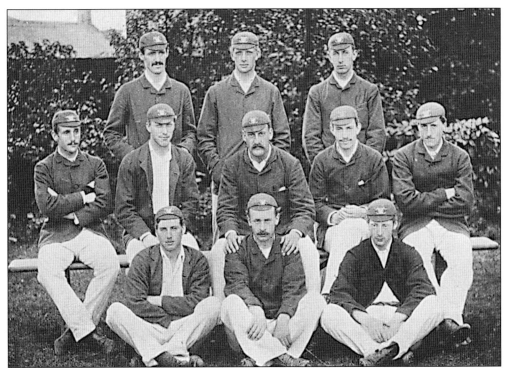

Oxford University XI in 1882. From left to right, back row: J.G. Walker, C.F.H. Leslie, G.E. Robinson. Middle row: A.O. Whiting, W.A. Thornton, N. MacLachlan (captain), M.C. Kemp, E.D. Shaw. Front row: W.D. Hamilton, E. Peake, J.I. Patterson.

Action from the Fenner's University Cricket Ground in 1882, with Cambridge University Cricket Club playing the touring Australians.

Cambridge University XI in 1882, who defeated Oxford in the Varsity Match at Lord's on 26, 27 and 28 June. From left to right, back row: R.C. Ramsey, Hon. M.B. Hawke, P.J. de Paravicini, F.E. Lacey, F.D. Gaddum. Front row: C.A. Smith, C.T. Studd, G.B. Studd (captain), C.W. Wright, J.E.K. Studd, P.J.T. Henery. Oxford totalled 165 and 257, Cambridge replying with 275 (G.B. Studd 120) and 148 for 3.

Oxford University XI in 1883. From left to right, back row: A.G.G. Asher, H.G. Ruggles-Birse, C.F.H. Leslie, T.R. Hine-Haycock, G.E. Robinson, H.V. Page. Front row: E. Peake, E.W. Bastard, M.C. Kemp (captain), W.E.T. Bolitho, J.G. Walker.

Cambridge University XI in 1883 who won the Varsity Match by 7 wickets. From left to right, back row: P.J. de Paravicini, J.A. Turner, H.G.T. Topham, P.J.T. Henery, W.N. Roe. Front row: C.W. Wright, J.E.K. Studd, C.A. Smith, C.T. Studd (captain), Hon. J.W. Mansfield, Hon. M.B. Hawke. The Varsity Match staged on 25, 26 and 27 June saw Cambridge total 215 (C.W. Wright 102) and 59 for 3, Oxford responding with 55 and 215. C.A. Smith took match figures of 9 for 106 for the light blues.

Born in Streatham, London in 1864, the cousin of L.H. Gay (Hampshire and Somerset), Kingsmill Key (Clifton and Oriel, Oxford), was an attacking middle order right-handed batsman and off-break bowler. He learnt his cricket at Clifton College in Bristol before going on to represent Oxford University between 1884 and 1887. He attained cricket blues all four years and in one year also attained a blue for rugby. He later entered county cricket with Surrey, and from 1882 to 1904 in 288 matches scored 9,654 runs (av. 26.23), with 8 hundreds and a highest score of 179. Whilst at Oxford, Key and H. Philipson added a record 340 partnership for the seventh wicket against Middlesex at Chiswick Park in 1887. During this match Key scored 281, the highest individual innings by a dark blue batsman in first-class cricket. Between 1894 and 1899 Key led Surrey to three championships. He toured abroad to North America twice in 1886 and 1891 and went to India in 1902/03 with the Oxford University Authentics. His last first-class appearance was in 1909, for H.D.G. Leveson-Gower's XI. He received a knighthood, and died in Wittersham, Kent in 1932 from blood poisoning after an insect bite.

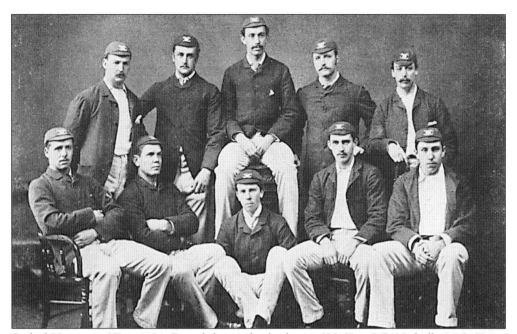

Oxford University XI in 1884. From left to right, back row: K.J. Key, B.E. Nicholls, M.C. Kemp (Captain), T.C. O'Brien, L.D. Hildyard. Front row: E.H. Buckland, H.V. Page, E.W. Bastard, H.O. Whitby, J.H. Brain. T.R. Hine-Haycock was absent at the time of the photograph. Oxford won the Varsity Match at Lord's on 30 June and 1 July, defeating Cambridge by a margin of 7 wickets. Cambridge reached 111 and 177. Oxford replied with 209 and 80 for 3.

Born in Dublin, Ireland in 1861, Timothy O'Brien (St. Charles' College, Notting Hill and New Inn Hall, Oxford), brother of J.G. (Ireland) and brother-in-law of C.E. de Trafford (Warwickshire and Leicestershire) was an attractive middle order right-handed batsman and useful left-arm bowler. He attended Downside School, before going on to Oxford University. He attained blues in both years, in 1884 and 1885. He later represented Middlesex in 156 matches between 1881 and 1898, scoring 7,377 runs (av. 29.63) with 10 hundreds and a top score of 202 for Middlesex versus Sussex at Hove in 1895. He also took 2 wickets (av. 136.00) and he held 111 catches and took 2 stumpings. He hit 1,000 runs in a season three times, with a best of 1,150 (av. 27.38) in 1884. Playing five Tests for England, one as captain, between 1884 and 1895/96, he scored 59 runs (av. 7.37) with a highest score of 20 and he held 4 catches. He toured abroad twice, with Vernon to Australia in 1887/88 and Lord Hawke to South Africa in 1895/96. He also represented Ireland in first-class matches between 1902 and 1907. He became Sir Timothy after succeeding to the barony on the death of his uncle. His last first-class match was for L. Robinson's XI, when he scored 90 and 111 in 1914. He died at Ramsay, Isle of Man in 1948.

Cambridge University XI in 1884. From left to right, back row: F. Marchant, C.W. Rock, J.A. Turner, H.G.T. Topham. Middle row: H.W. Bainbridge, C.A. Smith, J.E.K. Studd (captain), C.W. Wright, P.J. de Paravicini. Front row: Hon. J.W. Mansfield, D.G. Spiro.

Born in Ghowhatti, India in 1862, Herbert Bainbridge (Eton and Trinity, Cambridge) represented Cambridge University between 1884 and 1886 and captained the side in 1886. A right-handed opening batsman and slow round-arm bowler, he also represented Surrey (1883-85) in 11 matches, before representing the University – where he attained blues all three years. After leaving University, he represented Warwickshire between 1894 and 1902 in 118 matches and he toured America with Sanders' team in 1886. In total, Bainbridge played 177 first-class matches, scoring 6,878 runs (av. 25.76), with a top score of 162, bagged 31 wickets (av. 31.87), with a best haul of 3 for 21, and held 101 catches. Chairman and secretary of Warwickshire CCC, Bainbridge died at Leamington Spa in 1940.

Oxford University XI in 1885. From left to right, back row: E.H. Buckland, T.C. O'Brien, W.E.T. Bolitho, J.H. Brain, A.H.J. Cochrane. Middle row: E.W. Bastard, H.V. Page (captain), A.E. Newton, K.J. Key. Front row: H.O. Whitby, L.D. Hildyard.

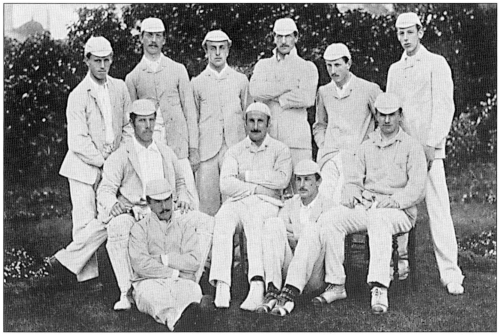

Cambridge University XI in 1885. From left to right, back row: C. Toppin, C.W. Rock, G.M. Kemp, C.A. Smith, F. Marchant, C.D. Buxton. Middle row: C.W. Wright, Hon. M.B. Hawke (captain), H.W. Bainbridge. Front row: P.J. de Paravicini, J.A. Turner. Cambridge defeated Oxford at Lord's on 29, 30 June and 1 July in the Varsity Match, by the margin of 7 wickets. The match details were: Oxford 136 and 239, Cambridge replying with 287 (H.W. Bainbridge 101) and 89 for 3.

Oxford University XI in 1886. From left to right, back row: A.H.J. Cochrane, H.T. Hewitt, A.R. Cobb, H.T. Arnall-Thompson, K.J. Key. Front row: W. Rashleigh, H.O. Whitby, H.V. Page (captain), J.H. Brain, L.D. Hildyard, E.H. Buckland. Oxford won the Varsity Match at Lord's on 5, 6 and 7 July, by 133 runs. The match details were: Oxford 191 and 304 (K.J. Key 143, W. Rashleigh 107), Cambridge 156 and 206.

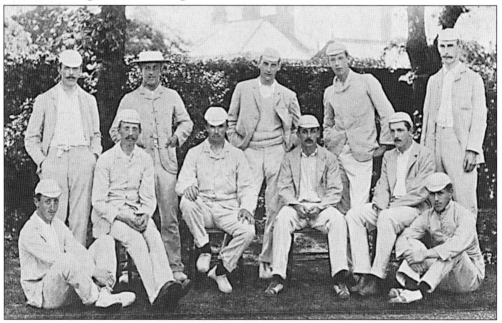

Cambridge University XI in 1886. From left to right, back row: Hon. C.M. Knatchbull-Hugessen, G.M. Kemp, L.A. Orford, C.D. Buxton, A.W. Dorman. Front row: F.F. Thomas, C.W. Rock, H.W. Bainbridge (captain), J.A. Turner, F. Marchant, C. Toppin.

Gilbert 'The Croucher' Jessop (Beccles, Cheltenham Grammar School and Christ's, Cambridge) was born in Cheltenham in 1874. An exceptional right-handed middle order batsman, right-arm fast bowler and good deep fielder, he represented Cambridge University between 1886 and 1899 and he captained the side in 1899. He played thirty-four games for Cambridge, scoring 1,391 runs (av. 27.27) with a top score of 171 not out. He took 127 wickets (av. 21.48) with a best haul of 8 for 34 and he held 29 catches. He later represented London County from 1900 to 1903 with Dr W.G. Grace's side based at Crystal Palace, and Gloucestershire between 1894 and 1914 in 345 games. He also played eighteen Tests for England from 1899 and 1912. In total he played 493 first-class matches, scored 26,698 runs (av. 32.63), with 53 centuries and a top score of 286 for Gloucestershire versus Sussex at Hove in 1903. He also collected 873 wickets (av. 22.79) with a best haul of 8 for 29 and he held 463 catches. He was captain of Gloucestershire between 1900 and 1912 and he also acted as secretary of the county from 1909 to 1912. He died in Fordington, Dorset in 1955.

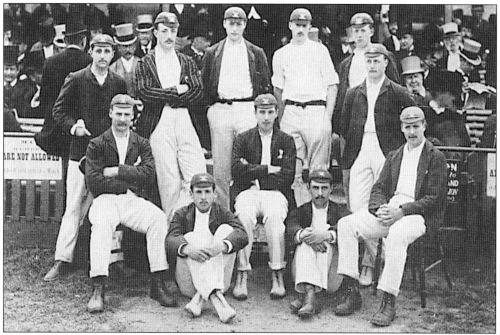

Oxford University XI in 1887. From left to right, back row: H. Philipson, G.W. Ricketts, H.W. Forster, Lord George Scott, E.A. Nepean, W. Rashleigh. Front row: K.J. Key, F.H. Gresson, J.H. Brain (captain), H.O. Whitby, E.H. Buckland. Victorious Oxford won the Varsity Match at Lord's on 4, 5 and 6 July by 7 wickets. Cambridge scored 207 and 252 (E. Crawley 103 not out), Oxford 313 (Lord George Scott 100) and 148 for 3.

Born in Paddington, London in 1866, Francis Ford (Repton and King's, Cambridge) was the son of W.A. (MCC 1839), brother of A.F.J. (Middlesex) and W.J. (Middlesex), nephew of G.J. (Oxford University), uncle of N.M. (Derbyshire and Middlesex) and great-uncle of J.R.T. Barclay (Sussex). An attractive left-handed middle order batsman, slow left-arm bowler and excellent slip fielder, he attended Repton School before going to Cambridge University. He attained blues in all four years between 1887 and 1890 and he captained the side in 1899. He made his Middlesex debut in 1886 and he represented them in 102 matches until 1899. He amassed 7,359 runs (av. 27.05) with 14 centuries and a top score of 191. He hit 1,000 runs in a season twice, with a best of 1,195 (av. 28.45) in 1899. He bagged 200 wickets (av. 23.78) with a best of 7 for 65 and he held 131 catches. He played five Tests for England in Australia in 1894/95, when he toured with Stoddart's team scoring 48 runs (av. 18.66) and taking a single wicket. His final first-class match was for an England XII in 1908. A noted goalkeeper, he was awarded a blue for soccer whilst at Cambridge. He died at Burwash, Sussex in 1940.

Cambridge University XI in 1887. From left to right, back row: H. Hale, F.G.J. Ford, L. Martineau, F. Meyrick-Jones. Middle row: F.F. Thomas, C. Toppin, F. Marchant (captain), C.D. Buxton, L.A. Orford. Front row: E. Crawley, W.C. Bridgeman. A.M. Sutthery was absent at the time the photograph was being taken.

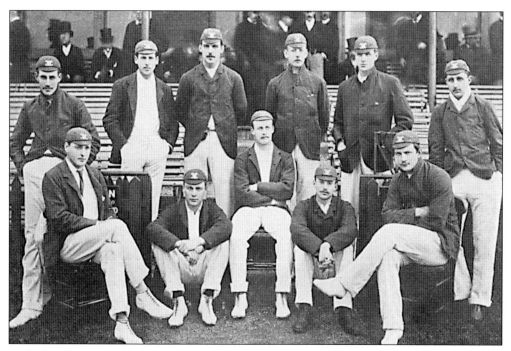

Oxford University XI in 1888. From left to right, back row: A.C.M. Croome, F.H. Gresson, G. Fowler, E.A. Nepean, Hon. F.J.N. Thesiger, H. Philipson. Front row: H.W. Forster, E.T.B. Simpson, W. Rashleigh (captain), Lord George Scott, A.H.J. Cochrane. The Varsity Match at Lord's on 2, 3, 4 and 5 July was drawn, Cambridge recording 171 and 170, Oxford with 124.

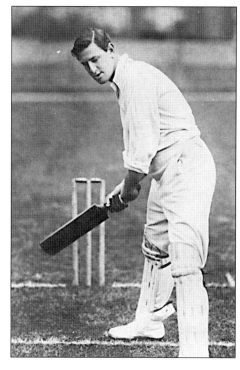

Sammy Woods (Brighton and Jesus, Cambridge) was born in Sydney, Australia in 1867. He represented Cambridge University, obtaining blues all four years between 1888 and 1891 and he captained the side in 1891. Woods played 28 matches for Cambridge, during which time he bagged 190 wickets (av. 14.93) with a best haul of 10 for 69 versus C.I. Thornton's XI at Fenner's in 1890, scored 837 runs (av. 20.92) with a best of 79 not out and he held 24 catches. He later represented Somerset from 1891 to 1910 in 299 matches and he also played Tests for both Australia (three in 1888) and England (three in 1895/96). During a career which saw him play a total of 401 first-class matches, he scored 15,345 runs (av. 23.42) with a highest score of 215 for Somerset versus Sussex at Hove in 1895, bagged 1,040 wickets (av. 20.82) and he held 279 catches. A useful rugby footballer and soccer player, he represented Cambridge University, Somerset and England as wing forward on the rugby pitch and for Sussex at soccer. He died in Taunton in 1931.

Cambridge University XI in 1888. From left to right, back row: H.J. Mordaunt, G. MacGregor, S.M.J. Woods, F.F. Thomas. Middle row: F.G.J. Ford, E.M. Butler, C.D. Buxton (captain), G.M. Kemp, R.C. Gosling. Front row: F. Meryrick-Jones, E. Crawley.

Oxford University XI in 1889. From left to right, back row: R.H. Moss, A.K. Watson, A.C.M. Croome, M.J. Dauglish. Middle row: F.H. Gresson, W. Rashleigh, H. Philipson (captain), H.W. Forster, Lord George Scott. Front row: H. Bassett, M.R. Jardine.

Born at Merchiston, Edinburgh, Scotland in 1869, Gregor MacGregor (Uppingham and Jesus, Cambridge) was a right-handed, lower order batsman and noted wicketkeeper. After Uppingham School he went on to Cambridge University, where he attained blues all four years between 1888 and 1891 and he captained the side in 1891. MacGregor made his Middlesex debut versus Lancashire in 1892 and he represented the county in 184 matches until 1907. For Middlesex he accumulated 4,846 runs (av. 19.61) with two hundreds and a top score of 141, and he held 280 catches and achieved 111 stumpings. He played eight Tests for England between 1890 and 1893, scoring 96 runs (av. 12.00) with a top score of 31 and he took 14 catches and 3 stumpings. He toured abroad twice, with Lord Sheffield to Australia in 1891/92 and with MCC to North America in 1907. He captained Cambridge University in 1891 and Middlesex from 1899 to 1907. A brilliant rugby footballer at full-back and centre, he represented Cambridge University in the Varsity matches of 1889 and 1890, and between 1889 and 1890 he represented his native Scotland in thirteen internationals. In 1890 he scored 131 out of a total of 730 for 9 declared for Cambridge University against Sussex, which was the highest second innings total in a first-class match in England. In his first season as Middlesex skipper Somerset were defeated inside just four hours and fifteen minutes. He was a Test selector in 1902, and from 1916 until his death was honorary treasurer of Middlesex CCC. He died in Marylebone, London in 1919.

Cambridge University XI in 1889. From left to right, back row: R.C. Gosling, H. Hale, F.F. Thomas, C.P. Foley. Middle row: H.J. Mordaunt, E.M. Butler, F.G.J. Ford (captain), S.M.J. Woods, G. MacGregor. Front row: E. Crawley, E.R. De Little. Cambridge won the Varsity Match at Lord's by the margin of an innings and 105 runs on 1 and 2 July. Oxford scored 105 and 90 with S.M.J. Woods recording match figures of 11 for 82, Cambridge 300 (H.J. Mordaunt 127).

Three

Varsity Blues

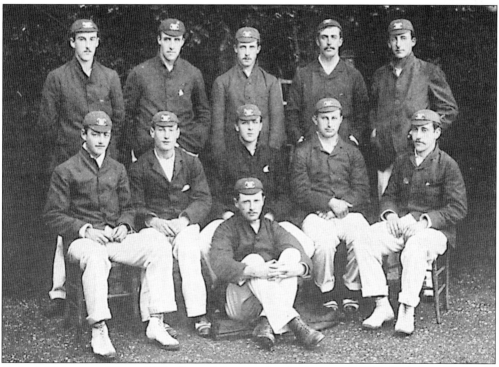

Oxford University XI in 1890. From left to right, back row: G.F.H. Berkeley, E. Smith, H.S. Schwann, G.L. Wilson, L.C.H. Palairet. Middle row: W.D. Llewellyn, M.R. Jardine, Hon. F.J.N. Thesiger (captain), H. Bassett, M.J. Dauglish. Front row: H.C. Bradley.

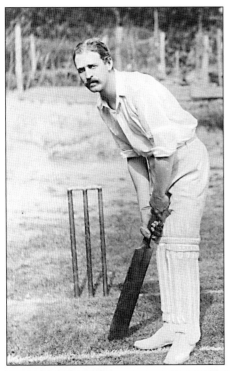

Born in Brixton in 1871, Digby Jephson (Manor House, Clapham and Peterhouse, Cambridge) was an opening batsman, right-arm fast-medium bowler who changed to under-arm lobs in 1892. He represented Cambridge University between 1890 and 1892, where he obtained blues in each year until he commenced his career with Surrey. Jephson played 24 matches for the University, scoring 525 runs (av. 17.50), bagged 7 wickets (av. 60.85) and he held 13 catches. He later represented Surrey in 165 matches from 1894 to 1904, scoring 6,566 runs (av. 32.02) with 9 centuries, including a highest score of 213 versus Derbyshire at Kennington Oval in 1900. He bagged 249 wickets (av. 23.08) with a best of 7 for 51 and he held 82 catches. Jephson achieved 1,000 runs in a season four times and his best season was 1900, when he amassed 1,952 runs (av. 41.53). He took over the captaincy of Surrey from K.J. Key, a former Oxford graduate, in 1900 before handing over the reigns to L. Walker in 1903. He died in Cambridge in 1926.

Cambridge University XI in 1890. From left to right, back row: D.L.A. Jephson, E.C. Streatfield, R.N. Douglas, F.S. Jackson, H. Hale, A.J.L. Hill. Front row: C.P. Foley, F.G.J. Ford, S.M.J. Woods (captain), R.C. Gosling, G. MacGregor. Cambridge were victorious by the margin of 7 wickets in the Varsity Match at Lord's on 30 June, 1 and 2 July thanks to match bowling figures of 8 for 56 by S.M.J. Woods. For the record, match details were: Oxford 42 and 108, Cambridge 97 and 54 for 3. Cambridge achieved their highest innings total in first-class matches, of 703 for 9 declared versus Sussex at Hove in 1890.

Lionel Palairet (Repton and Oriel, Oxford) was born in Grange-over-Sands, Lancashire in 1870. He represented Oxford University between 1890 and 1893, attaining blues in all four years and captaining the side between 1892 and 1893. He was a stylish right-handed batsman and right-arm medium bowler, occasionally bowling under-arm lobs, and he went on to represent Somerset. He played for the county from 1891 to 1909, during which time he played 222 games. He also played two Tests for England in 1902 versus Australia, scoring 49 runs (av. 12.25). In a total of 267 first-class matches he accumulated 15,777 runs (av. 33.63) with 27 hundreds and a highest innings of 292 for Somerset versus Hampshire at Southampton in 1896. He also bagged 143 wickets (av. 33.90) and he held 248 catches and took 15 stumpings. A good all-round sportsman, he played soccer for the Corinthians and he also represented Oxford in athletics. He died in Exmouth, Devon in 1933.

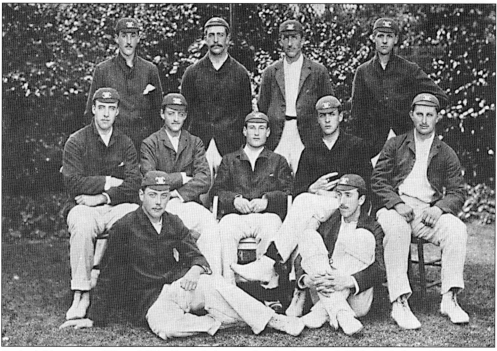

Oxford University XI in 1891. From left to right, back row: G.F.H. Berkeley, G.L. Wilson, L.C.H. Palairet, A.J. Boger. Middle row: E. Smith, W.D. Llewellyn, M.R. Jardine (captain), Hon. F.J.N. Thesiger, H. Bassett. Front row: H.D. Watson, W.H. Brain. T.B. Case was absent when the photograph was taken.

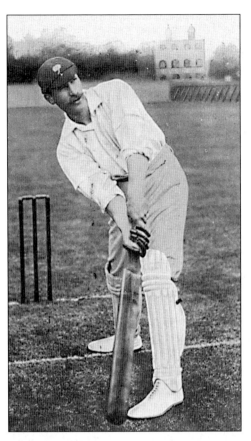

Rt. Hon. Sir Francis Stanley Jackson (Harrow, Trinity College Cambridge) was born in Leeds in 1870. He represented Cambridge University between 1890 and 1893 and he captained the light blues between 1892 and 1893 before he represented Yorkshire and England. Jackson played 35 matches for Cambridge, scoring 1,649 runs (av. 26.59). He took 153 wickets (av. 17.73) with a best haul of 8 for 54 and he held 23 catches. He represented Yorkshire between 1890 and 1907 in 207 matches and played twenty Tests for England from 1893 to 1905. In total Jackson played 309 first-class matches and as a stylish right-handed batsman he scored 15,901 runs (av. 33.83) with a highest score of 160, bagged 774 wickets (av. 20.37) with his right-arm medium fast bowling and he held 195 catches. He died in Knightsbridge, London in 1947.

Born at St. Pancras, London in 1871, brother of L.S. (Middlesex) and Clifford (Cambridge University), Cyril Wells (Dulwich and Trinity, Cambridge), was an attractive right-handed middle order batsman, off and leg break bowler and fine slip fielder. He attained blues in all three years between 1891 and 1893 while at Cambridge University. He played four matches for Surrey between 1892 and 1893 before moving to Lord's in 1895. He represented Middlesex 113 times between 1895 and 1909. During his career he accumulated 4,229 runs (av. 22.02) with four centuries, including a top score of 244 for Middlesex versus Nottinghamshire at Trent Bridge, Nottingham in 1899. He bagged 465 wickets (av. 19.86), with a best performance of 8 for 35 and he held 122 catches. A well-respected rugby footballer, he represented Cambridge University, Harlequins, Middlesex and England. He died at St. John's Wood, London in 1963.

Cambridge University XI in 1891. From left to right, back row: W.I. Rowell, E.C. Streatfield, C.M. Wells, G.J.V. Weigall. Middle row: C.P. Foley, F.S. Jackson, G. MacGregor (captain), S.M.J. Woods, R.N. Douglas. Front row: D.L.A. Jephson, A.J.L. Hill. Cambridge won the Varsity Match by 2 wickets at Lord's on 29 and 30 June. Cambridge scored 210 and 93 for 8, Oxford 108 and 191. S.M.J. Woods recorded match figures of 11 for 112 in the match for the light blues.

Oxford University XI in 1892. From left to right, back row: T.S.B. Wilson, V.T. Hill, J.B. Wood, C.B. Fry. Middle row: W.H. Brain, M.R. Jardine, L.C.H. Palairet (captain), G.F.H. Berkeley, T.B. Case. Front row: F.A. Phillips, R.T. Jones. Oxford won the Varsity Match at Lord's on 30 June 1 and 2 July by 5 wickets. Oxford made 365 (M.R. Jardine 140, V.T. Hill 114) and 187 for 5, Cambridge 160 and 388 (E.C. Streatfield 116).

Cambridge University XI in 1892. From left to right, back row: H.R. Bromley-Davenport, G.J.V. Weigall, P.H. Latham, L.H. Gay. Middle row: R.N. Douglas, A.J.L. Hill, F.S. Jackson (captain), C.M. Wells, E.C. Streatfield. Front row: D.L.A. Jephson, J. Douglas.

Charles B. Fry (Repton and Wadham, Oxford) was born in West Croydon, Surrey in 1872. Fry represented Oxford University between 1892 and 1895 and during the 1894 season he captained the side with distinction. An exceptional right-handed top order batsman, right-arm fast-medium bowler and fielder, he later went on to represent Sussex in 236 matches between 1894 and 1908, before moving to Hampshire, whom he represented between 1909 and 1921. Fry also represented London County between 1900 and 1902 and he toured abroad with Lord Hawke to South Africa in 1895/96. He played twenty-six Tests for England between 1895/86 and 1912. An Oxford triple blue, Fry was also a noted athlete and soccer player representing Southampton in the 1902 FA Cup final and for England versus Ireland in 1901. In total he played 394 first-class matches, scoring 30,886 runs (av. 50.22) with 94 centuries and a highest score of 258 not out. He also bagged 166 wickets (av. 29.34) with a best haul of 6 for 78, and he held 240 catches. He died in Hampstead, London in 1956.

Born in Chelford, Cheshire in 1870, Hugh Bromley-Davenport (Eton and Trinity, Cambridge) represented Cambridge University between 1892 and 1893. He played seventeen matches for the University whilst scoring 286 runs (av. 16.82), took 48 wickets (av. 36.31) and he held 7 catches for the light blues. He later played 28 matches for Middlesex from 1896 to 1898 and represented England in four Tests between 1895/96 and 1898/99. During his career he played a total of 76 first-class matches, scoring 1,801 runs (av. 18.37), took 187 wickets (av. 17.92) with a best performance of 7 for 17 and he held 48 catches. He died in South Kensington, London in 1954.

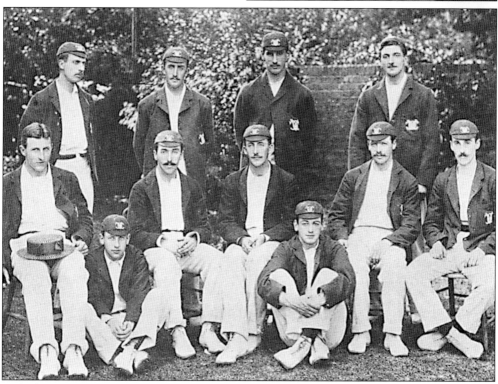

Oxford University XI in 1893. From left to right, back row: R.W. Rice, R.C.N. Palairet, G.J. Mordaunt, C.B. Fry. Middle row: J.B. Wood, W.H. Brain, L.C.H. Palairet (captain), T.S.B. Wilson, G.F.H. Berkeley. Front row: H.D.G. Leveson-Gower, L.C.V. Bathurst.

Gerald Mordaunt (Wellington and University, Oxford) was born in Wellesbourne, Warwickshire in 1873. He represented Oxford University between 1893 and 1896, won blues in all four years and he captained the side in 1895. He later played 16 matches for Kent between 1895 and 1897 and toured with Lord Hawke's XI to North America in 1894. He played 60 first-class matches, scored 2,675 runs (av. 26.22) – with a top score of 264 not out for Oxford University versus Sussex at Hove in 1895 – and he held 72 catches. A useful athlete, he represented Oxford in the long jump. He died at Hayling Island, Hampshire in 1959.

Cambridge University XI in 1893, who defeated Oxford by 266 runs in the Varsity Match at Lord's on 3 and 4 July. From left to right, back row: A.O. Jones, L.H. Gay, T.T.N. Perkins, K.S. Ranjitsinhji. Middle row: C.M. Wells, P.H. Latham, F.S. Jackson (captain), A.J.L. Hill, E.C. Streatfield. Front row: J. Douglas, H.R. Bromley-Davenport. Match details were: Cambridge 182 and 254, with Oxford responding with 106 and 64.

Born in India in 1872, K.S. Ranjitsinhji (Rajkumar College, India and Trinity, Cambridge)
'Ranji' represented Cambridge University in 1893 and 1894, during which time he
represented the light blues ten times. He scored 427 runs (av. 30.50), with a top score of 58,
and he held 20 catches. He also played 211 matches for Sussex from 1895 to 1920, London
County 1901 to 1904, and England in fifteen Tests from 1896 to 1902. In total he played 307
first-class matches and amassed 24,692 runs (av. 56.37) with a top score of 285 not out for
Sussex versus Somerset at Taunton in 1901. He also took 133 wickets (av. 34.59) and he held
233 catches. He died in India in 1933.

Oxford University XI in 1894. From left to right, back row: R.P. Lewis, G.B. Raikes, G.R. Bardswell, D.H. Forbes. Middle row: G.J. Mordaunt, L.C.V. Bathurst, C.B. Fry (captain), R.C.N. Palairet, H.D.G. Leveson-Gower. Front row: F.A. Phillips, H.K. Foster. The Varsity Match at Lord's on 2, 3 and 4 July was won by Oxford by 8 wickets. Oxford achieved 338 (C.B. Fry 100 not out) and 88 for 2, Cambridge 222 and 200.

Born at Titsey Place, Surrey in 1873, Henry 'Shrimp' Leveson-Gower (Winchester and Magdalen, Oxford), was a right-handed middle order batsman, leg-break bowler and good cover fielder. Learning his early cricket whilst at Winchester, he progressed to Oxford University where he obtained blues in all four years between 1893 and 1896. Leveson-Gower later represented Surrey in 122 matches between 1895 and 1920. He captained Oxford in 1896 and Surrey between 1908 and 1910 and he led MCC to South Africa in 1909/10. He played three Tests on that tour, scoring 95 runs (av. 23.75). Leveson-Gower, during later life, ran his own first-class cricket XI, and after retiring he became a noted cricket administrator, including periods as a Test selector and committee member and he was president of Surrey CCC from 1929 to 1939. In 1953 he was knighted for his services to cricket. He died in Kensington, London in 1954.

The 1894 Cambridge University XI. From left to right, back row: N.F. Druce, J.J. Robinson, E. Field, C.G. Pope. Middle row: F. Mitchell, J. Douglas, P.H. Latham (captain), T.T.N. Perkins, W.G. Druce. Front row: J. Du V. Brunton, H. Gray.

C.J. BURNUP. (KENT)

Born in Blackheath, Kent in 1875, Cuthbert James Burnup (Malvern and Clare, Cambridge) attended Malvern School, and Cambridge University between 1895 and 1898, attaining blues in 1896, 1897 and 1898 as a sound top order right-handed batsman, slow right-arm bowler and good fielder. He represented Kent in 157 matches between 1896 and 1907, scoring 9,668 runs (av. 38.06) with a top score of 200 versus Lancashire at Old Trafford, Manchester in 1900. He took 41 wickets (av. 43.78) with a best performance of 5 for 44 and he held 74 catches. He also represented London County under W.G. Grace in 1901 and toured abroad, with Plum Warner in 1898 and Lord Hawke in 1902/03. He died in Golders Green, London in 1960.

Born in Trinidad in 1873, 'Plum' Warner (Rugby and Oriel, Oxford), captained Rugby School before making his first-class debut for Oxford University in 1894, where he gained blues in 1895 and 1896. A right-handed batsman, he played for Middlesex from 1894 to 1920 and he acted as captain from 1908 to 1920. Playing a total of 519 first-class matches, he scored 29,028 runs with 60 centuries and recorded a top score of 244 for the Rest of England versus Warwickshire at Kennington Oval in 1911. For England he played fifteen Tests from 1898/99 to 1912 and he scored 622 runs with a best of 132 not out for England against South Africa at Johannesburg in 1898/99. Few cricketers have dedicated so much of their life to the game of cricket as 'Plum', in his capacity as player, manager, Test selector, writer and founder of *The Cricketer* magazine in 1921. He was knighted for his services to cricket in 1937. He acted as deputy secretary of MCC during the Second World War, became president in 1950/51 and he had a stand named after him at Lord's in 1958. He died in West Lavington, Sussex in 1953 and his ashes were scattered at Lord's near the spot where he hit his first four.

Preb. Archdale Palmer Wickham was born at South Holmwood, Surrey in 1855. The uncle of B.N.B. (Middlesex), he was educated at Marlborough and was a specialist wicketkeeper and right-handed lower order batsman. He played Minor County cricket for Norfolk between 1882 and 1890 and he represented Oxford University from 1876 to 1878, attaining a blue in 1878. He later represented Somerset 82 times from 1891 to 1907. In total he played 93 matches, scoring 760 runs (av. 8.83) with a top score of 28 and he achieved 150 dismissals (91 catches and 59 stumpings). He acted as president of Somerset CCC and he died in East Brent, Highbridge, Somerset in 1935.

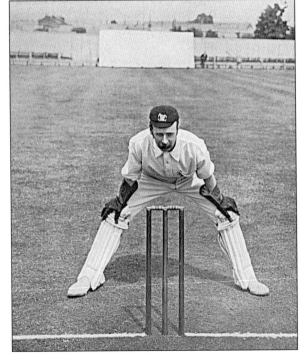

Born in Denmark Hill, London in 1872, Walter Druce (Marlborough and Cambridge) was the brother of N.F. (Surrey) and the cousin of E.A.C. (Kent). A right-handed middle order batsman, wicketkeeper and good cover point fielder, he represented Cambridge University between 1894 and 1895, attaining a blue both years. Captain of Cambridge in 1895, he also played rugby for his University and his final first-class match was in 1913 for the MCC. He played a total of 39 matches, scoring 1,568 (av. 28.00) with 3 centuries and a highest score of 129. As a wicketkeeper he achieved 52 dismissals (47 catches and 5 stumpings). He died in Sherborne, Dorset in 1963.

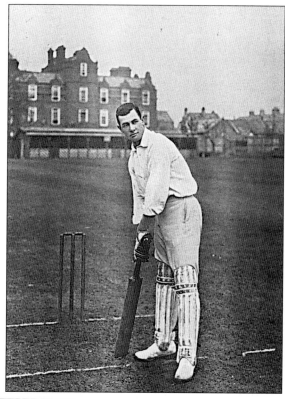

Alexander Eccles (Repton and Oxford) was born in Ashton-on-Ribble, Lancashire in 1876. He attended Repton School and learnt his early cricket there before moving down to Oxford University in 1896. He represented the dark blues between 1896 and 1899, achieving a blue in his last three years. He later went on to represent his native Lancashire as a right-handed batsman and good fielder in 123 matches between 1898 and 1907. His best season was 1899, when he amassed 1,070 runs (av. 26.09). In total he played in 152 matches, scoring 5,129 runs (av. 23.20) with 6 centuries and a highest innings of 139. He also took 1 wicket (av. 88.00) with a best of 1 for 17 and he held 95 catches. He died suddenly whilst ploughing at Bilsborough Hall near Preston in Lancashire in 1919.

Francis Stocks (Lancing, Denstone, Oxford) was born in Market Harborough, Leicestershire in 1873. A left-handed lower order batsman, left-arm medium pace bowler and good fielder, he went to school at Lancing and Denstone before moving to Oxford University in 1896. He represented his native Leicestershire from 1894 to 1903 44 times and Oxford University from 1896 to 1899, attaining blues in his latter two years. He toured abroad once, going to North America in 1897 with Pelham Warner. In total he played 63 matches, scoring 834 runs (av. 10.04) with a top score of 58, bagged 208 wickets (av. 25.02) with a best haul of 8 for 22 and he held 70 catches. He also won a blue for hockey whilst at Oxford. He died at Framlingham, Suffolk in 1929.

The 1895 Oxford University XI. From left to right, back row: R.P. Lewis, H.A. Arkwright, G.B. Raikes, G.O. Smith. Middle row: F.A. Phillips, H.D.G. Leveson-Gower, G.J. Mordaunt (captain), C.B. Fry, H.K. Foster. Front row: P.F. Warner, F.H.E. Cunliffe. Oxford recorded their highest innings total of 651 versus Sussex at Hove in 1895.

Cambridge University XI in 1895. From left to right, back row: H. Gray, J. Burrough, W.G. Grace, W.W. Lowe. Middle row: C.E.M. Wilson, F. Mitchell, W.G. Druce (captain), N.F. Druce, R.A. Studd. Front row: H.H. Marriott, W.M. Hemingway. Cambridge won the 1895 Varsity Match at Lord's, staged between 4 and 6 July, by 134 runs. Cambridge scored 244 and 288, Oxford 202 and 196 (H.K. Foster 121).

University Parks Cricket Ground, Oxford in 1896.

Oxford University XI in 1896. From left to right, back row: F.H.E. Cunliffe, J.C. Hartley, P.S. Waddy, G.O. Smith. Middle row: H.K. Foster, G.R. Bardswell, H.D.G. Leveson-Gower (captain), G.J. Mordaunt, R.P. Lewis. Front row: P.F. Warner, C.C. Pilkington. 'Shrimp' Leveson-Gower led Oxford to a 4-wicket victory in the Varsity Match at Lord's on 2, 3 and 4 July. Match details were: Cambridge 319 and 212, Oxford 202 and 330 for 6 (G.O. Smith 132).

CAMBRIDGE UNIVERSITY CRICKET GROUND. Photo by Stearn & Son, Cam

Fenner's Cricket Ground, Cambridge in 1896.

Cambridge University XI in 1896. From left to right, back row: H.H. Marriott, E.B. Shine, W.G. Grace, P.W. Cobbold. Middle row: W.M. Hemingway, N.F. Druce, F. Mitchell (captain), C.F.M. Wilson, E.H. Bray. Front row: C.J. Burnup, G.L. Jessop.

Born in Ireland in 1875, Frederick Fane (Charterhouse and Magdalen, Oxford), represented Oxford University between 1896 and 1898 and he attained blues between 1897 and 1898. Schooled at Charterhouse, Fane was a right-handed opening batsman who later represented Essex in 292 matches between 1895 and 1922. In total he amassed 18,548 runs (av. 27.39), with a top score of 217 for Essex versus Surrey at Kennington Oval in 1911. He also represented London County in 1901 and England in fourteen Tests between 1905/06 and 1909/10. His final first-class appearance was for H.D.G. Leveson-Gower's XI in 1924 and he died at Brentwood, Essex in 1960.

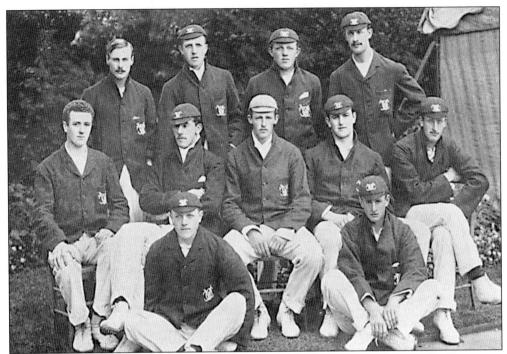

Oxford University XI in 1897. From left to right, back row: F.L. Fane, F.H.B. Champain, A. Eccles, E.C. Wright. Middle row: P.S. Waddy, F.H.E. Cunliffe, G.R. Bardswell (captain), J.C. Hartley, G.E. Bromley-Martin. Front row: R.W. Fox, R.E. Foster.

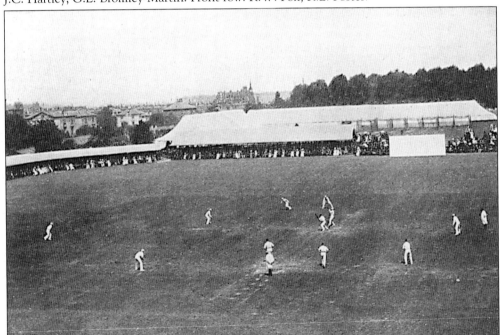

Lord's viewed from the Pavilion. Oxford University versus Cambridge University Varsity Match in 1897, with R.E. Foster and A. Eccles batting for Oxford University, whilst Cambridge University are in the field.

Reginald Foster (Malvern, University College Oxford) was born in Malvern in 1878. He represented Oxford University between 1897 and 1900, attaining blues in all four years, and he captained the dark blues during his final season 1900 at the University Parks. He later represented Worcestershire in 80 games from 1899 to 1912 and he played eight Tests for England from 1903/04 to 1907. In total he played 139 first-class matches, scored 9,076 runs (av. 41.82) with a highest score of 287 for England versus Australia at Sydney in 1903/04, bagged 25 wickets (av. 46.12) and he held 179 catches. A useful sportsman, he won blues whilst at Oxford in soccer, golf and rackets and he represented Corinthians and England at soccer. He died in Kensington, London of diabetes in 1914.

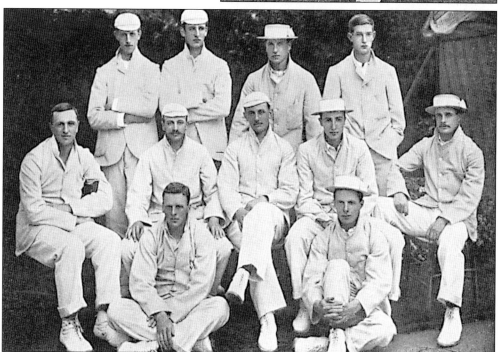

Cambridge University XI in 1897, who defeated Oxford in the Varsity Match, staged at Lord's between 5 and 7 July, by 179 runs. From left to right, back row: J.H. Stogdon, H.W. De Zoete, E.B. Shine, A.E. Fernie. Middle row: F. Mitchell, C.E.M. Wilson, N.F. Druce (captain), H.H. Marriott. Front row: E.H. Bray, C.J. Burnup. Cambridge accumulated 156 and 336, Oxford 162 and 151.

Tom Taylor (Uppingham and Trinity, Cambridge) was born in Leeds in 1878. He represented Cambridge University between 1898 and 1900 and captained the side in 1900. Taylor represented Cambridge thirty times, accumulating 1,221 runs (av. 25.43) with a top score of 120. He held 26 catches and took 2 stumpings. He later played 82 matches for Yorkshire from 1899 to 1906. He also played hockey and tennis at Cambridge. He died in Leeds in 1960.

Born at Bulls Cross, Enfield in 1877, Bernard Bosanquet (Eton and Oriel, Oxford) was a tall medium-pace right-arm leg-break bowler and a hard-hitting batsman, who invented the 'googly'. He represented Oxford University from 1898 to 1900 and he then joined Middlesex, whom he represented between 1889 and 1919. He played 123 first-class matches, scored 11,696 runs with 21 centuries and took 629 wickets. He achieved the coveted double in 1904, and became the first to complete a match double of a hundred in each innings and an aggregate of 10 wickets, in the same match for Middlesex versus Sussex at Lord's in 1905. He hit 214 in 195 minutes while playing for the Rest of England versus Yorkshire at Kennington Oval in 1908. Playing seven Tests for England between 1903/04 and 1905, he took 25 wickets with a best performance of 8 for 107 versus Australia at Trent Bridge, Nottingham in 1905. He toured abroad three times and while at University he gained half-blues at billiards and hammer throwing and was also a fine ice-hockey player. Father of the late Reginald Bosanquet of television news fame, he died at Ewhurst, Surrey in 1936.

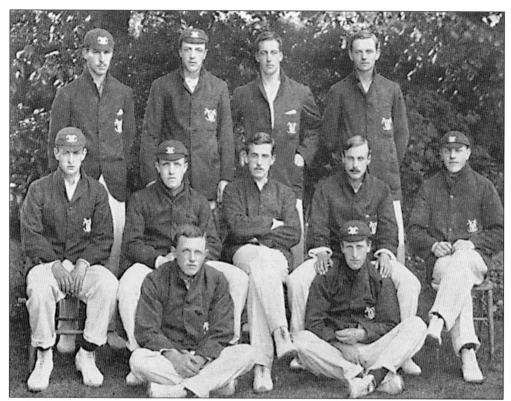

Oxford University XI in 1898. From left to right, back row: E.C. Lee, B.J.T. Bosanquet, R.D. Bannon, F.W. Stocks. Middle row: R.E. Foster, F.H.B. Champain, F.H.E. Cunliffe (captain), F.L. Fane, R.W. Fox. Front row: A. Eccles, G.E. Bromley-Martin. Oxford defeated Cambridge in the Varsity Match at Lord's by 9 wickets on 30 June and 1 and 2 July. Cambridge scored 273 (C.E.M. Wilson 115) and 140, Oxford 362 (A. Eccles 109 not out) and 52 for 1.

Lord's Cricket Ground, pictured during the luncheon interval of the Varsity Match in 1898.

Lord's viewed from the pavilion during the Varsity Match in 1898. R.E. Foster is batting for Oxford University, with Cambridge University in the field.

Cambridge University XI in 1898. From left to right, back row: A.T. Coode, G.E. Winter, H.H.B. Hawkins, C.J. Burnup. Middle row: G.L. Jessop, J.H. Stogdon, C.E.M. Wilson (captain), H.W. De Zoete, H.H. Marriott. Front row: A.E. Hind, T.L. Taylor.

Born in Bayswater, London in 1879, Richard Blaker (Westminster and Jesus, Cambridge) represented Cambridge University between 1899 and 1902, attaining blues in 1900, 1901 and 1902. He played 29 matches for Cambridge, scoring 1,030 runs (av. 22.39) with a top score of 79 not out. He later represented Kent in 119 matches from 1898 to 1908. In total he played 162 first-class matches, totalled 5,359 runs (av. 22.61) with a highest score of 122 and he held 143 catches. He died in Eltham, Kent in 1950.

Cambridge University Cricket Club seen here in action versus the touring Australians at Fenner's University Cricket Ground, Cambridge in 1899.

Oxford University XI in 1899. From left to right, back row: H.C. Pilkington, R.H. De Montmorency, H. Martyn, A.M. Hollins. Middle row: B.J.T. Bosanquet, R.E. Foster, F.H.B. Champain (captain), A. Eccles, F.W. Stocks. Front row: L.P. Collins, F.P. Knox. The Varsity Match at Lord's staged on 3, 4 and 5 July was drawn. Oxford made 192 and 347, Cambridge 241 and 229 for 4.

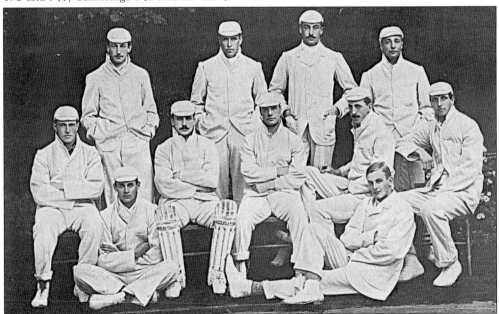

Cambridge University XI in 1899. From left to right, back row: A.E. Hind, L.J. Moon, E.F. Penn, J. Daniell. Middle row: G.E. Winter, T.L. Taylor, G.L. Jessop (captain), J.H. Stogdon, H.H.B. Hawkins. Front row: S.H. Day, E.R. Wilson.

Francis H.B.(Bateman) Champain (Cheltenham, Oxford) was born in Richmond, Surrey in 1877. The brother of C.E., H.F. and J.N. (all Gloucestershire) and nephew of F. Currie (Gentlemen of Kent), F.L. Currie (Cambridge University), R.G. Currie (Gentlemen of Surrey and Sussex) and brother-in-law of F.A. Currie (MCC). He was a stylish right-handed top order batsman, slow right-arm bowler and good fielder. He played 83 matches for Gloucestershire between 1895 and 1914 and Oxford University from 1897 to 1900, attaining blues all four years. In 1899 he captained Oxford and whilst at University he also won a blue for rugby. In total he played 114 matches, scoring 4,677 runs (av. 24.61) with 5 hundreds and a highest score of 149. He also achieved 17 wickets (av. 24.58) with a best haul of 6 for 62 and he held 101 catches. He died in Tiverton, Devon in 1942.

Born in Penge, London in 1881, Edward Dillon (Rugby and University, Oxford) attained blues at Oxford in both years of 1901/02. A hard-hitting left-hander and useful leg-break bowler, he made his debut for Kent in 1900. In the same season he also represented the London County Club at Crystal Palace, scoring 108 on his debut against Worcestershire for the side which was led and organised by Dr W.G. Grace. A notable rugby footballer, he played three-quarter for both Blackheath and England. For Kent he played 223 matches, until his retirement from the game in 1923. He scored 9,415 runs (av. 28.88) with a top score of 141, bagged 27 wickets (av. 48.92) with a best performance of 3 for 20 and he 195 catches. He toured the West Indies with Bennett's side in 1901/02 and with Kent to North America in 1903. He died in Totteridge, Hertfordshire in 1941.

Four

The Golden Age

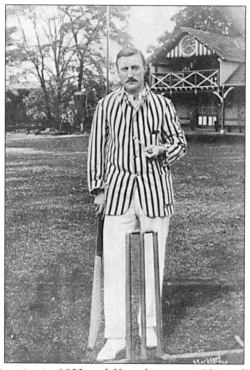

Captain of Oxford University in 1902 and Kent between 1904 and 1908, Henry Marsham (Eton and Christ Church, Oxford) was born in Bicester, Oxfordshire in 1879. Playing his early cricket at Eton and Oxford University, he attained blues in all three years between 1900 and 1902 and he later represented Kent between 1900 and 1922 in 141 matches. A sound middle order batsman, he scored 4,397 runs (av. 20.93) with a highest innings of 128 for Kent versus Essex at Tonbridge in 1908, and he held 74 catches. His best county season was 1904, when he amassed 1,070 runs (av. 28.91). He later played Minor County cricket for Shropshire and was a Test selector in 1907. He died at Wrotham Hill, Kent in 1928.

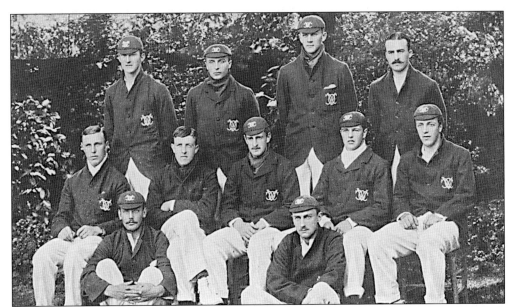

Oxford University XI in 1900. From left to right, back row: C.D. Fisher, J.W.F. Crawfurd, H. White, H.C. Pilkington. Middle row: H. Martyn, F.H.B. Champain, R.E. Foster (captain), F.P. Knox, B.J.T. Bosanquet. Front row: R.E. More, C.H.B. Marsham. B.J.T. Bosanquet achieved a record haul of 15 for 65 in a match versus Sussex at the University Parks during the 1900 season. Oxford University recorded their highest innings total of 503 against Cambridge University in 1900.

Cambridge University XI in 1900. From left to right, back row: J. Stanning, J. Daniell, E.M. Dowson, R.N.R. Blaker. Middle row: E.R. Wilson, S.H. Day, T.L. Taylor (captain), L.J. Moon, A.E. Hind. Front row: A.H.C. Fargus, A.E. Fernie. Staged at Lord's between 5 and 7 July, the Varsity Match between the light and dark blues was drawn. Oxford made 503 (R.E. Foster 171) and 219 for 6 declared, Cambridge 392 and 186 for 2.

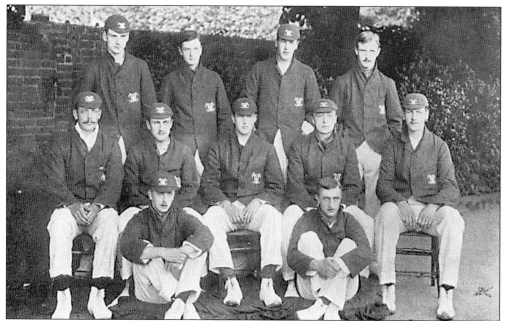

Oxford University XI in 1901. From left to right, back row: W. Findlay, R.A. Williams, E.W. Dillon, H.J. Wyld. Middle row: R.E. More, C.H.B. Marsham, F.P. Knox (captain), J.W.F. Crawfurd, G.W.F. Kelly. Front row: J.S. Munn, F.H. Hollins. Staged at Lord's between 4 and 6 July, the Varsity Match between the light and dark blues was drawn. Cambridge scored 325 (E.R. Wilson 118) and 337, Oxford 336 and 177 (C.H.B. Marsham 100 not out).

Cambridge University XI in 1901. From left to right, back row: W.P. Robinson, P.R. Johnson, J. Daniell, R.N.R. Blaker. Middle row: A.H.C. Fargus, E.R. Wilson, S.H. Day (captain), E.M. Dowson, A.E. Hind. Front row: L.V. Harper, H.K. Longman.

Oxford University XI in 1902. From left to right, back row: W.S. Medlicott, W.H.B. Evans, A.C. von Ernsthausen, R.A. Williams. Middle row: E.W. Dillon, W. Findlay, C.H.B. Marsham (captain), H.J. Wyld, G.W.F. Kelly. Front row: R.C.W. Burn, M. Bonham-Carter.

Cambridge University XI in 1902, who won the Varsity Match at Lord's staged between 3 and 5 July. From left to right, back row: R.N.R. Blaker, C.E. Winter, L.T. Driffield, J. Gilman, F.B. Wilson. Middle row: S.H. Day, E.M. Dowson, E.R. Wilson (captain), L.V. Harper, E.F. Penn. Front row: C.H.M. Ebden. Match details were: Oxford 206 and 254 – with E.M. Dowson recording match figures of 10 for 166 – Cambridge 186 and 274 for 5 (S.H. Day 117 not out).

The Pavilion at Fenner's University Cricket Ground, Cambridge in 1902.

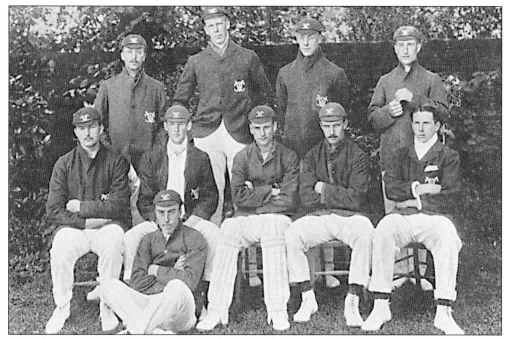

Oxford University XI in 1903. From left to right, back row: K.M. Carlisle, E.G. Martin, J.E. Raphael, A.C. Pawson. Middle row: A.C. von Ernsthausen, W.H.B. Evans, W. Findlay (captain), H.J. Wyld, R.C.W. Burn. Front row: O.M. Samson. C.D. McIvor was absent at the time of the photograph. Oxford won the Varsity Match by 268 runs at Lord's between 2 and 4 July. Oxford reached 259 (J.E. Raphael 130) and 291, Cambridge 137 and 145, with W.H.B. Evans recording match figures of 11 for 86 for the dark blues.

Lord's viewed from the Nursery End during the Oxford University versus Cambridge University Varsity Match in 1903. Seen here are J.E. Raphael and K.M. Carlisle batting for Oxford University, with Cambridge University in the field.

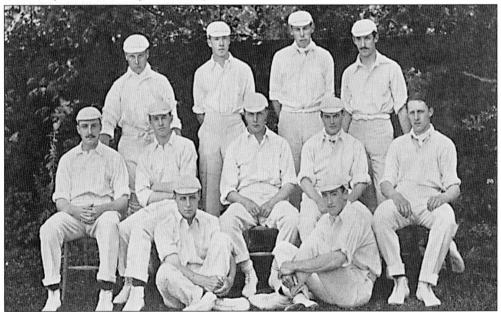

Cambridge University XI in 1903. From left to right, back row: G.M. Buckston, F.B. Roberts, G. Howard-Smith, H.C. McDonell. Middle row: E.W. Mann, L.V. Harper, E.M. Dowson (captain), C.H.M. Ebden, F.B. Wilson. Front row: R.P. Keigwin, R.T. Godsell.

Oxford University XI in 1904. From left to right, back row: J.E. Raphael, L.D. Brownlee, R.W. Awdry, G.T. Branston. Middle row: R.G.W. Burn, K.M. Carlisle, W.H.B. Evans (captain), A.C. von Ernsthausen, E.G. Martin. Front row: C.D. McIvor, W.S. Bird.

Born in Brussels, Belgium in 1882, John 'Jack' Raphael (Merchant Taylors' and St. John's, Oxford) was an attacking right-handed opening batsman and slow medium right-arm bowler. He learnt his early cricket whilst at Merchant Taylors' School, before going up to St. John's College, Oxford. He attained blues for cricket whilst at Oxford University in 1903, 1904 and 1905. He later represented Surrey in 39 matches between 1903 and 1909, scoring 1,614 runs (av. 28.31) with a highest score of 111; he also held 15 catches. He captained Surrey during the latter part of the 1904 season and also played for Dr W.G. Grace for London County in 1901 and 1902. Raphael's best season was 1904, when he scored 1,695 runs (av. 39.41) with a career best 201 for Oxford University versus the mighty Yorkshire at the University Parks. During the Varsity matches of 1903, 1904 and 1905, Raphael scored 130, 19, 12, 25, 99 and 6 at Lord's. A full England rugby football international, he won nine caps at three-quarter-back. He also stood as a Liberal candidate for Croydon but was not elected. He died at Remy, Belgium in 1917 from wounds received in the Battle of Messines Ridge and he is buried near Poperinge in Belgium.

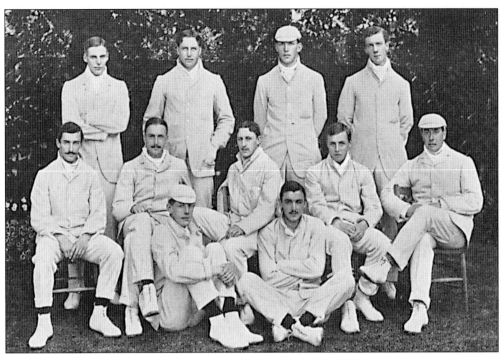

Cambridge University XI in 1904. From left to right, back row: E.S. Phillips, F.J.V.B. Hopley, K.R.B. Fry, C.H. Eyre. Middle row: H.C. McDonell, E.W. Mann, F.B. Wilson (captain), R.P. Keigwin, J.F. Marsh. Front row: G.G. Napier, M.W. Payne. The 1904 Varsity Match at Lord's was drawn. Cambridge made 253 and 390 (J.F. Marsh 172 not out), Oxford 149 and 221 for 6, with H.C. McDonell recording match figures of 9 for 135.

The Hon. C.N. Bruce (Winchester and New, Oxford) was born in London in 1885. Clarence Bruce was succeeded to the title 3rd Baron Aberdare in 1929. A right-handed hard-hitting, middle order batsman, he attended Winchester School, before attending University. He represented Oxford University from 1905 to 1908, attaining blues in 1907 and 1908. He later made his Middlesex debut in 1908 and played 62 times for the county until 1929. He scored 4,326 runs (av. 29.03) with a top score of 149 and he held 34 catches. An excellent rackets player, he was the amateur champion in 1922 and 1931 and was doubles champion on ten occasions. He represented Oxford University at both rackets and golf, and for over twenty years worked for the International Olympic Executive. He also played cricket for Wales from 1925 to 1929. He died when the car in which he was travelling went over a precipice into a river near Kotor in Yugoslavia, in 1957.

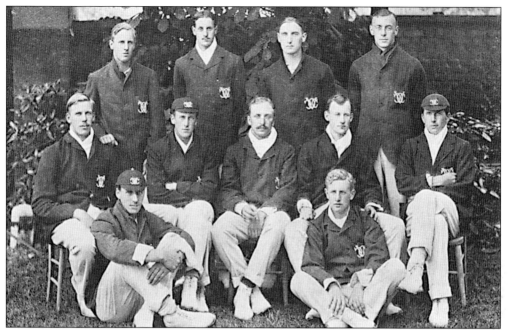

Oxford University XI in 1905. From left to right, back row: E.L. Wright, G.T. Branston, N.R. Udal, J.E. Raphael. Middle row: E.G. Martin, W.S. Bird, K.M. Carlisle (captain), W.H.B. Evans, R.C.W. Burn. Front row: F.A.H. Henley, G.N. Foster.

The Cambridge University XI who defeated Oxford in the Varsity Match at Lord's on 6, 7 and 8 July 1905. From left to right, back row: C.C. Page, G.G. Napier, A.F. Morcom, P.R. May. Middle row: M.W. Payne, C.H. Eyre, E.W. Mann (captain), H.C. McDonell, R.P. Keigwin. Front row: R.A. Young. L.G. Colbeck was absent at the time the photograph was taken. Cambridge made 218 and 264 (L.G. Colbeck 107), Oxford 319 (J.E. Raphael 99, E.L. Wright 95) and 123. A.F. Morcom recorded match figures of 9 for 110 for the light blues.

Born in Dharwar, India in 1885, Robert Young (Repton and King's, Cambridge) represented Cambridge University between 1905 and 1908, attaining blues all four years, and he captained Cambridge in 1908. He represented Cambridge 36 times, during which time he amassed 2,254 runs (av. 35.21) with a highest score of 150; he also took 1 for 28 with the ball and he held 2 catches. A good right-handed batsman and wicketkeeper, he attended Repton School before moving to Cambridge and after leaving University he played for Sussex in 86 matches from 1905 to 1925. He also played two Tests for England on tour in Australia in 1907/08. In total he played 139 first-class matches, scored 6,653 runs (av. 28.80) with a highest score of 220 for Sussex versus Essex at Leyton in 1905, and he held 115 catches and achieved 29 stumpings. A useful soccer outside right, Young represented Cambridge University and the Corinthian Casuals. He died in Hastings, Sussex in 1968.

Oxford University XI in 1906. From left to right, back row: R.V. Buxton, W.J.H. Curwen, J.H. Gordon, G.N. Foster. Middle row: G.T. Branston, E.L. Wright, W.S. Bird (captain), E.G. Martin, N.R. Udal. Front row: Hon. R.G. Barnes, C.A.L. Payne.

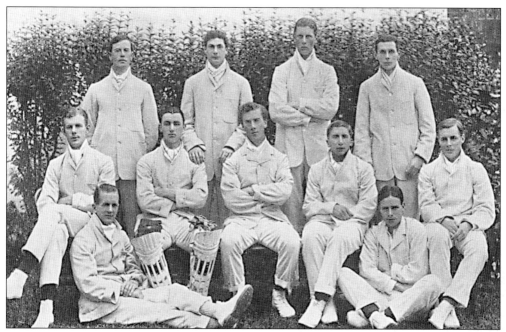

Cambridge University XI in 1906. From left to right, back row: A.F. Morcom, C.C. Page, J.N. Buchanan, L.G. Colbeck. Middle row: G.G. Napier, M.W. Payne, C.H. Eyre (captain), R.A. Young, R.P. Keigwin. Front row: H. Mainprice, P.R. May. Cambridge won the Varsity Match at Lord's on 5, 6 and 7 July by 94 runs. Cambridge reached 360 (R.A. Young 150) and 248 for 6 declared, Oxford 187 and 327.

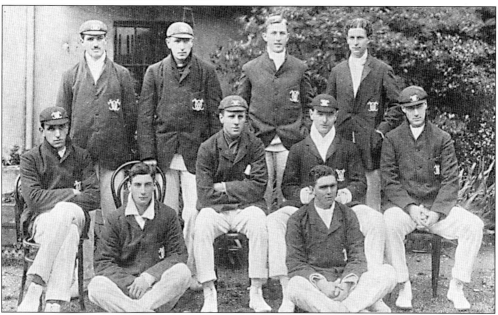

Oxford University XI in 1907. From left to right, back row: Hon. C.N. Bruce, H.A. Gilbert, T. Bowring, J.C.M. Lowe. Middle row: C.A.L. Payne, E.L. Wright (captain), J.H. Gordon, Hon. R.G. Barnes. Front row: D.R. Brandt, C.S. Hurst. G.N. Foster was absent at the time the photograph was taken.

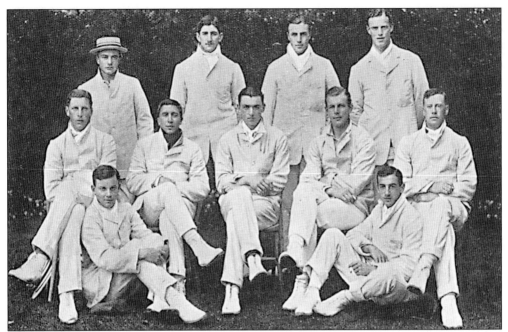

Cambridge University XI in 1907. From left to right, back row: W.P. Harrison, H.J. Goodwin, F.H. Mugliston, C. Palmer. Middle row: J.N. Buchanan, R.A. Young, M.W. Payne (captain), G.G. Napier, A.F. Morcom. Front row: A.D. Finlay, C.C.G. Wright. Winning the Varsity Match at Lord's staged on 4, 5 and 6 July by 5 wickets, Oxford recorded 141 and 112, with Cambridge responding with 108 and 146 for 5. A.F. Morcom and G.G. Napier both recorded 9 wicket hauls in the match, for 98 and 104 respectively.

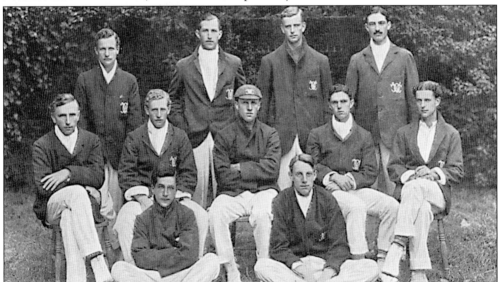

Oxford University XI in 1908. From left to right, back row: H. Teesdale, T. Bowring, R.L. Robinson, Hon. C.N. Bruce. Middle row: H.A. Gilbert, G.N. Foster, E.L. Wright (captain), C.S. Hurst, J.C.M. Lowe. Front row: A.G. Pawson, C.E. Hatfield. Oxford won the Varsity Match by 2 wickets. Cambridge attained 188 and 201, Oxford 207 and 183 for 8, despite E. Olivier taking match figures of 10 for 141 for the light blues.

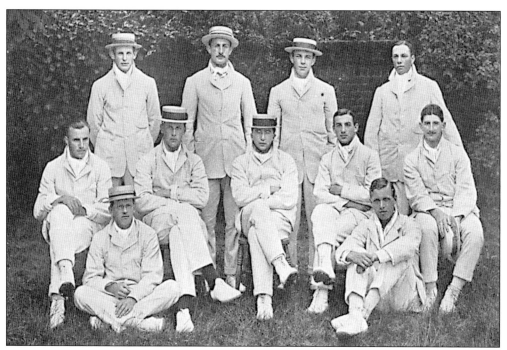

Cambridge University XI in 1908. From left to right, back row: Hon. C.F. Lyttelton, R.E.H. Baily, K.G. Macleod, E. Olivier. Middle row: F.H. Mugliston, J.N. Buchanan, R.A. Young (captain), C.C.G. Wright, H.J. Goodwin. Front row: J.F. Ireland, M. Falcon.

Born at Winchmore Hill, Middlesex in 1888, Frank Mann (Malvern and Pembroke, Cambridge) learnt his early cricket at Malvern in Worcestershire before playing for Cambridge University from 1908 to 1911. A lusty right-handed batsman and occasional right-arm slow bowler, he represented Middlesex from 1909 to 1931 (1921 to 1928 as captain), winning a famous championship at his first attempt in 1921. He played 398 first-class matches, scoring 13,235 runs with 9 centuries and with a top score of 194. Captaining England in his five Tests versus South Africa in 1922/23, he won 14 of the 22 tour matches, including the Test series 2-1 with wins at Cape Town and Durban. He scored 281 runs during the series, with a top score of 84 in the third Test at Durban; he later became a Test selector in 1930 and subsequently became president of Middlesex MCC. He died at Milton-Lilbourne, Wiltshire in 1964.

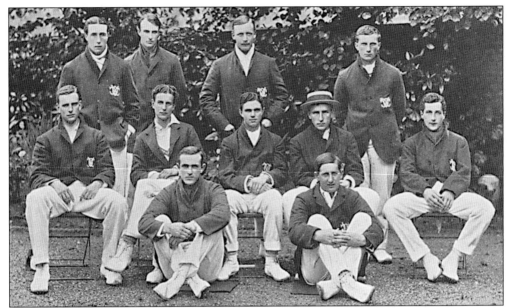

Oxford University XI in 1909. From left to right, back row: C.V.L. Hooman, A.J. Evans, R.O. Lagden, M.G. Salter. Middle row: R.L. Robinson, J.C.M. Lowe, C.S. Hurst (captain), H.A. Gilbert, A.G. Pawson. Front row: P.R. Le Couteur, J.A. Seitz. The Varsity Match was drawn at Lord's on 5, 6 and 7 July. Oxford made 267 and 191, Cambridge 183 and 89 for 4.

Guy Pawson, seen here keeping wicket on the beach whilst his son Tony is batting, was born in Bramley, Leeds in 1888. He went to school at Winchester before going up to Christ Church, Oxford, representing the University between 1908 and 1911. He attained blues in all four years and he was captain of the side in 1910, thirty-eight years ahead of his son H.A. 'Tony', who captained the side in 1948. A lower-order right-handed batsman and wicketkeeper, Guy Pawson shared with W.G. Keighley a record second wicket partnership of 226 versus Cambridge University at Lord's in 1947. After graduating from Oxford, Pawson played a single match for Worcestershire in 1908. In total he played 28 first-class games, scored 448 runs (av. 12.10) and he achieved 46 dismissals (30 catches and 16 stumpings). He died in Lamerton, Devon in 1986.

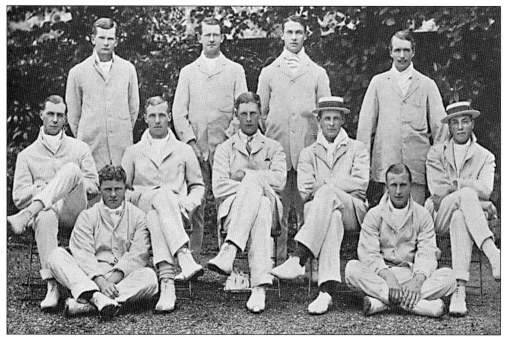

Cambridge University XI in 1909. From left to right, back row: J.H.B. Lockhart, J.F. Ireland, F.T. Mann, N.C. Tufnell. Middle row: K.G. Macleod, M. Falcon, J.N. Buchanan (captain), Hon. C.F. Lyttelton, E. Olivier. Front row: J.W.W. Nason, H.E.W. Priest.

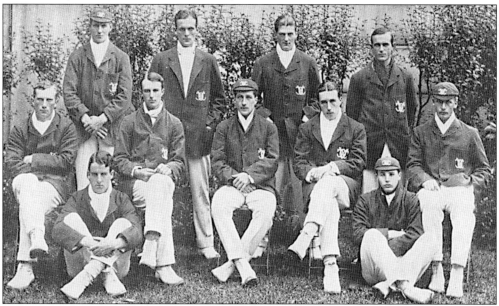

The Oxford University XI, who won the Varsity Match known as 'Le Couteur's match' at Lord's by the huge margin of an innings and 126 runs in 1910. From left to right, back row: R. Sale, R.L.L. Braddell, F.N. Tuff, P.R. Le Couteur. Middle row: M.G. Salter, A.J. Evans, A.G. Pawson (captain), C.V.L. Hooman, R.O. Lagden. Front row: J.L.S. Vidler, R.H. Twining. The match details were: Oxford 315 (P.R. Le Couteur 160), Cambridge 76 and 113, with P.R. Le Couteur recording match figures of 11 for 66 for the dark blues.

Alfred Evans (Winchester and Oriel, Oxford) represented Oxford University between 1909 and 1912 and he captained the University side in 1911. Born in Newtown, Hampshire in 1899, he represented Kent between 1921 and 1928 in 36 matches. A right-handed batsman and bowler, he scored 1,303 runs (av. 25.05) with a top score of 143 versus Lancashire at Maidstone in 1927 and he took 19 wickets (av. 31.84) and he held 41 catches. His nephew, brother and cousin all played for Hampshire, where he originally commenced his career, although he only played 7 matches for Hampshire between 1908 and 1920. He also attained blues every year whilst at Oxford University between 1909 and 1912, and he played a single Test for England in 1921. He captained Oxford University in 1911 and Kent in 1927 and during the First World War he won achieved fame for his escapes from German POW camps. He died in Marylebone, London in 1960.

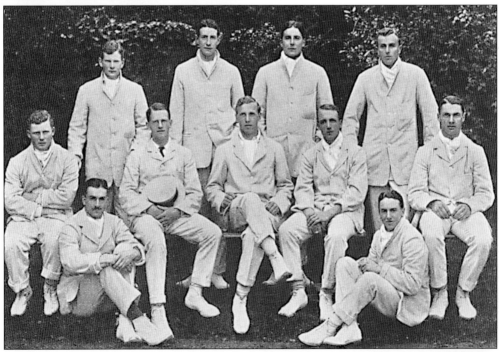

Cambridge University XI in 1910. From left to right, back row: J.H.B. Lockhart, O. Hughes, A.G. Cowie, D.C. Collins. Middle row: J.W.W. Nason, J.F. Ireland, M. Falcon (captain), N.C. Tufnell, F.T. Mann. Front row: E.L. Kidd, N.J. Holloway.

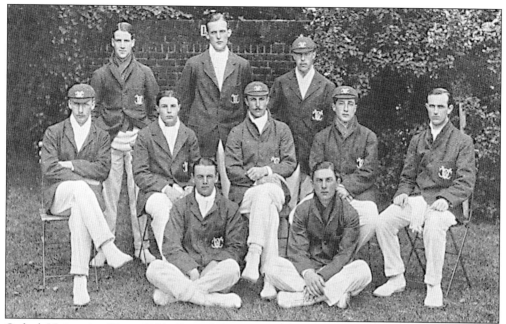

Oxford University XI in 1911. From left to right, back row: J.L.S. Vidler, R.L.L. Braddell, H.S. Altham. Middle row: R.O. Lagden, R.H. Twining, A.J. Evans (captain), A.G. Pawson, P.R. Le Couteur. Front row: H. Brougham, I.P.F. Campbell. R.V. Bardsley was absent at the time the photograph was taken. Oxford won the Varsity Match by 74 runs at Lord's between 3 and 5 July. Match details were: Oxford 203 and 328, Cambridge 217 and 240. P.R. Le Couteur recorded match figures of 11 for 179 for the dark blues.

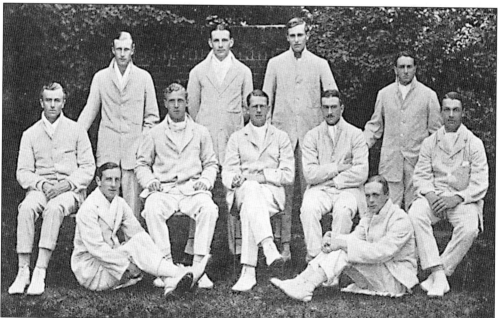

Cambridge University XI in 1911. From left to right, back row: H.E.W. Priest, H. Grierson, Hon. H.G.H. Mulholland, N.J. Holloway. Middle row: D.C. Collins, M. Falcon, J.F. Ireland (captain), E.L. Kidd, F.T. Mann. Front row: S.H. Saville, M.E.C. Baggalay.

Born in Kensington, London in 1892, the Hon. Frederick Calthorpe (Repton and Jesus, Cambridge) represented Cambridge University between 1912 and 1914 and again in 1919. He later represented Warwickshire from 1919 to 1930 in 231 matches and England in four Tests in 1929/30. Calthorpe represented Cambridge 40 times, scoring 1,234 runs (av. 20.56) with a top score of 88. He also bagged 117 wickets (av. 22.17) with a best of 5 for 43 and he held 24 catches. He died in Worplesdon, Surrey in 1935.

Fully printed-up scorecard of the Freshmen's Match staged at Fenner's University Cricket Ground on Saturday 4 May 1912.

Fully printed up scorecard of the First XII versus Next XVI match staged at Fenner's University Cricket Ground on Wednesday 8 May 1912.

Camb. University Cricket Ground.
WEDNESDAY, MAY 8, 1912.
FIRST XII. v. NEXT XVI.

N.B.—In each Innings the Players go in as their names appear on the Card.

MR. A. H. LANG'S SIDE. — 1st inns. / 2nd inns.

	1st inns.	2nd inns.
1 Mr. A. H. Lang (Trin.), b Smythe	0	lbw, b Holloway ... 25
2 Mr. R. G. Tudor (Sel.), b Smythe	2	b Calthorpe ... 7
3 Mr. G. W. V. Hopley (Trin.), b Kidd	36	cWoosnam,bMulholland 9
16 Mr. J. S. F. Morrison (Trin.), b Holloway	0	c Calthorpe, b W.-Clive 44
9 Mr. R. B. Lagden (Pemb.), c Arnold, b Holloway	5	b Smythe ... 59
10 Mr. A. J. Wood (Cath.), c Patteson, b Holloway	3	b Knight ... 53
8 Mr. G. A. Fairbairn (Jes.), b Kidd	27	run out ... 5
13 Hon. G. J. Mulholland (Trin.), b Holloway	7	st Arnold, b Patterson 66
15 Mr. R. H. Fowler (Trin.), c Patteson, b Kidd	8	cW.-Clive,bMulholland 47
7 Mr. H. G. Vincent (Jes.), st Arnold, b Kidd	8	c Knight, b Calthorpe 19
5 Mr. L. W. Bridges (Sel.), lbw, b Kidd	8	c Arnold, b Calthorpe 0
4 Mr. B. P. Nevile (Trin.), run out	1	b Calthorpe ... 23
6 Mr. J. H. Falcon (Pemb.), b Holloway	15	cWoosnam,bCalthorpe 11
12 Mr. K. King (Clare), st Arnold, b Mulholland	2	not out ... 1
11 Mr. E. C. Baker (Cath.), not out	2	b Calthorpe ... 0
14 Mr. J. W. Mason (Caius), c W.-Clive, b Mulholland	0	b Riley ... 0
Extras	2	Extras ... 38
Total	**120**	**Total ... 372**

Wkts	1	2	3	4	5	6	7	8	9	10	11	12	13	14	15
Runs, 1st inns.	0	7	9	19	35	71	74	86	89	91	94	106	118	120	120
" 2nd inns.	21	41	50	68	164	181	206	295	328	328	336	367	371	372	

MR. E. L. KIDD'S SIDE. — 1st inns. / 2nd inns.

	1st inns.	2nd inns.
2 Hon. H. G. H. Mulholland (Trin.), b Mason	70	c Fairbairn, b Falcon 2
10 Mr. C. Patteson (Pemb.), c Mulholland, b Falcon	24	c Lang, b Baker ... 14
7 Mr. R. Knight (Christ's), c Lang, b Baker	0	lbw, b Bridges ... 44
6 Mr. W. N. Riley (Cath.), c Fairbairn, b Falcon	1	b Bridges ... 44
4 Mr. M. J. Susskind (Pemb.), c Baker, b Nevile	72	c Mulholland, b Fowler 23
1 Mr. E. L. Kidd (Pemb.), b Nevile	6	b Bridges ... 0
8 Mr. M. Woosnam (Trin.), c Hopley, b Baker	1	b Fowler ... 6
11 Hon. A. Windsor-Clive (Trin.), c and b Nevile	29	c Mulholland, b Fowler 4
5 Mr. F. S. G. Calthorpe (Jes.), b Nevile	0	st Lang, b Falcon ... 15
3 Mr. N. J. Holloway (Jes.), c Lagden, b Falcon	10	not out ... 31
12 Mr. A. C. P. Arnold (Magd.), c Morrison, b Nevile.	0	not out ... 42
9 Mr. D. Smythe (Jes.), not out	0	
Extras	15	Extras ... 25
Total	**228**	**Total ... 246**

Wkts	1	2	3	4	5	6	7	8	9	10		1	2	3	4	5	6	7	8	9	10
Runs	0	59	63	140	160	161	193	202	206	216	2	26	105	127	127	142	149	154	176		

Umpires—E. Mignon and J. O'Connor.

Play will commence First Day at 12, other two days at 11.30. Luncheon, First Day, 2—2.45; other two days, 1.30—2.15. Stumps drawn at 6.30.

MATCHES TO COME.
May 9, 10, 11—University v. Middlesex.
May 16, 17, 18—University v. Sussex.
May 20, 21, 22—Perambulators v. Etceteras.
May 23, 24, 25—University v. Yorkshire.
June 3, 4, 5—UNIVERSITY v. SOUTH AFRICANS.*
June 6, 7, 8—UNIVERSITY v. AUSTRALIANS.*
June 10, 11, 12—University v. Free Foresters.
* Free Admission to Ladies will be suspended at these three Matches.

D. M. HAYWARD (Custodian), DEALER in all kinds of CRICKET GOODS. BATS from the BEST MAKERS.

Hy. Smith, Printer, 58, Devonshire Road, Cambridge.

Cambridge University Cricket Ground, June 5, 1912.
University v. South Africans.

N.B.—In each Innings the Players go in as their names appear on the Card.

THE UNIVERSITY. — 1st inns. / 2nd inns.

	1st inns.	2nd inns.
10 Mr. R. Knight, c Beaumont, b Carter	66	b Schwarz ... 16
9 Mr. W. N. Riley, b Faulkner	1	b Faulkner ... 49
2 Mr. C. Patteson, lbw, b Faulkner	1	st Stricker, b Schwarz ...
4 Hon. H.G.H. Mulholland, c Nourse, b Faulkner	8	b Faulkner ... 5
7 Mr. J. H. B. Sullivan, b Faulkner	1	b Carter ... 13
1 Mr. E. L. Kidd, b Faulkner	14	c Snooke, b Carter ... 31
5 Mr. S. H. Saville, c Snooke, b Carter	8	st Stricker, b Faulkner ...
9 Mr. F. S. G. Calthorpe, b Carter	4	b Faulkner ... 3
6 Hon. G. J. Mulholland, b Carter	6	not out ... 3
8 Mr. N. J. Holloway, not out	5	lbw, b Carter ... 0
11 Mr. A. C. P. Arnold, c Hartigan, b Carter	10	c Hartigan, b Faulkner ... 11
Extras	9	Extras ... 4
Total	**130**	**Total ... 182**

Wkts	1	2	3	4	5	6	7	8	9	10		1	2	3	4	5	6	7	8	9	10
Runs	19	20	22	28	64	89	97	108	113	130	63	63	66	73	105	166	118	118	119	182	

SOUTH AFRICANS. — 1st inns. / 2nd inns.

	1st inns.	2nd inns.
2 Mr. G. P. D. Hartigan, lbw, b Calthorpe	38	not out ... 2
3 Mr. H. W. Taylor, lbw, b Calthorpe	36	not out ... 1
4 Mr. A. D. Nourse, c Holloway, b H. Mulholland	6	
5 Mr. S. J. Snooke, c G. J., b H. Mulholland	8	
6 Mr. G.A. Faulkner, cHolloway,bH. Mulholland	6	
1 Mr. J. Tancred, st Arnold, b Holloway	94	
8 Mr. R.O.Schwarz, c H. Mulholland,b Holloway	11	
10 Mr. L. A. Stricker, c Kidd, b Calthorpe	42	
9 Mr. R. Beaumont, b Sullivan	10	
11 Mr. C. P. Carter, b Sullivan	0	
7 Mr. J. L. Cox, not out	1	
Extras	10	Extras ...
Total	**260**	**Total ...**

Wkts	1	2	3	4	5	6	7	8	9	10		1	2	3	4	5	6	7	8	9	10
Runs	70	77	82	91	98	130	222	244	244	260											

Umpires—W. Richards and J. Moss.

Play will commence First Day at 12, other two days at 11.30. Luncheon, First Day, 2—2.45; other two days, 1.30—2.15. Stumps drawn at 6.30.

MATCHES TO COME.
June 6, 7, 8—UNIVERSITY v. AUSTRALIANS.*
June 10, 11, 12—University v. Free Foresters.
* Free Admission to Ladies will be suspended at these Matches.

NOW READY.]   FORTIETH ANNUAL ISSUE OF   [TWOPENCE.

SMITH'S 'LIGHT BLUE' BOAT RACE CARD
WITH PLAN OF THE COURSE,
Names and Colours of the Crews, Order of Starting, Daily Register and Chart of Bumps, Particulars of Racing, Trains to and from Barnwell Junction, ENTRANCE FEES TO DITTON PADDOCK AND GRAND STAND, etc.

D. M. HAYWARD (Custodian), DEALER in all kinds of CRICKET GOODS. BATS from the BEST MAKERS.

Fully printed up scorecard of the Cambridge University versus South Africans tour match staged at Fenner's University Cricket Ground on 5 June 1912.

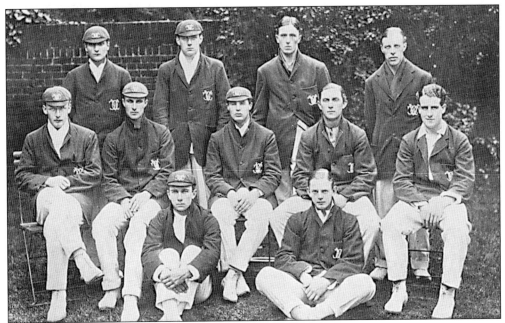

Oxford University XI in 1912. From left to right, back row: G.E.V. Crutchley, R.V. Bardsley, E.A. Shaw, H.S. Altham. Middle row: R.O. Lagden, A.J. Evans, R.H. Twining (captain), I.P.F. Campbell, J.L.S. Vidler. Front row: J.N. Fraser, F.H. Knott.

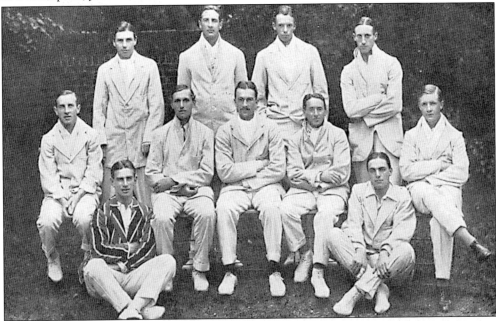

Cambridge University XI in 1912. From left to right, back row: J.S.F. Morrison, G.W.V. Hopley, E.C. Baker, Hon. F.S.G. Calthorpe. Middle row: S.H. Saville, Hon. H.G.K. Mulholland, E.L. Kidd (captain), N.J. Holloway, R.B. Lagden. Front row: W.N. Riley, W.B. Franklin. Cambridge beat Oxford by 3 wickets in the Varsity Match staged at Lord's between 1 and 3 July. Oxford made 221 (G.E.V. Crutchley 99 not out) and 213, Cambridge 221 and 214 for 7.

William Wilkinson (Eton and University, Oxford) was born in Sydney, Australia in 1892. A right-handed top order batsman and slow right-arm bowler, he represented Oxford University in 1913 and 1914, attaining a blue in 1913. He later toured Australia and New Zealand with MCC in 1922/23 and played a total of 89 first-class matches, scoring 4,785 runs (av. 31.48) with a top score of 129. He also took 12 wickets (av. 32.08) with a best of 4 for 32 and he held 49 catches. He won a blue for athletics whilst at Oxford, and he died in Storrington, Sussex in 1983.

Cambridge University XI in 1913. From left to right, back row: A.H. Lang, W.B. Franklin, E.C. Baker, G.A. Fairbairn, B.S. Cumberlege, R. Du. B. Evans. Front row: K.H.C. Woodroffe, E.L. Kidd, S.H. Saville, Hon. H.G.H. Mulholland (captain), R.B. Lagden, Hon. F.S.G. Calthorpe, G.B. Davies.

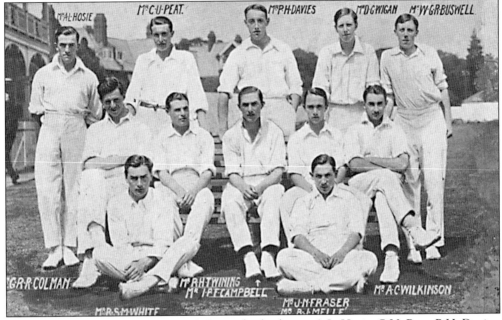

Oxford University XI in 1913. From left to right, back row: A.L. Hosie, C.U. Peat, P.H. Davies, D.G. Wigan, W.G.R. Buswell. Front row: G.R.R. Colman, R.S.M. White, R.H. Twining, I.P.F. Campbell (captain), J.N. Fraser, B.J. Melle, A.C. Wilkinson.

Born in Sutton, Surrey in 1894, Donald Knight (Malvern and Trinity, Oxford) was a stylish right-handed opening batsman and excellent close fielder. He learnt his early cricket whilst at Malvern, where he captained the school XI in 1912 and 1913. He also captained the Public Schools XI at Lord's and, like Miles Howell, he obtained blues at Oxford in 1914 and 1919. He later represented Surrey from 1911 to 1937 and played 107 matches for the county, accumulating 4,390 runs (av. 29.66) with 9 hundreds and a highest innings of 146. Although joining the teaching profession, which limited his first-class cricket appearances for Surrey after University, his best season was in 1919, when he amassed 1,588 runs (av. 45.37). He also represented England in two Tests in 1921 against Australia, achieving a top score of 38. He died in Marylebone, London in 1960.

Fully printed up scorecard of the Cambridge University versus Yorkshire match, staged at Fenner's on 29 May 1914.

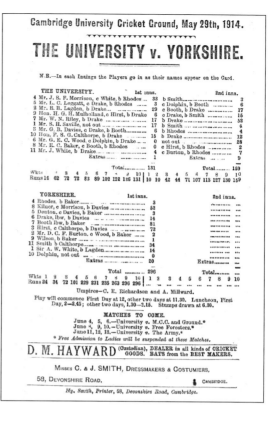

Cambridge University Cricket Ground, May 29th, 1914.

THE UNIVERSITY v. YORKSHIRE.

N.B.—In each Innings the Players go in as their names appear on the Card.

THE UNIVERSITY.	1st inns.		2nd inns.
4 Mr. J. S. F. Morrison, c White, b Rhodes	33	b Smith	3
5 Mr. L. C. Leggatt, c Drake, b Rhodes	3	c Dolphin, b Booth	6
2 Mr. R. B. Lagden, b Drake	29	c Booth, b Drake	17
9 Hon. H. G. H. Mulholland, c Hirst, b Drake	6	c Drake, b Smith	15
7 Mr. W. N. Riley, b Drake	17	b Drake	52
1 Mr. S. H. Saville, not out	17	b Smith	4
3 Mr. G. B. Davies, c Drake, b Booth	6	b Rhodes	4
10 Hon. F. S. G. Calthorpe, b Drake	15	b Drake	12
6 Mr. G. E. C. Wood, c Dolphin, b Drake	0	not out	28
8 Mr. E. C. Baker, c Booth, b Rhodes	0	c Hirst, b Rhodes	2
11 Mr. J. White, b Drake	4	c Burton, b Rhodes	7
Extras	1	Extras	9
Total	131	Total	159

Wkts 2 3 4 5 6 7 8 9 10 | 1 2 3 4 5 6 7 8 9 10
Runs 14 62 72 72 83 89 102 122 126 131 | 10 10 42 44 71 107 113 127 130 159

YORKSHIRE.	1st inns.		2nd inns.
4 Rhodes, b Baker	3	...	...
8 Kilner, c Morrison, b Davies	52	...	...
5 Denton, c Davies, b Baker	3	...	...
6 Drake, lbw, b Davies	14	...	...
7 Booth, lbw, b Baker	81	...	...
3 Hirst, c Calthorpe, b Davies	72	...	...
2 Mr. D. C. F. Burton, c Wood, b Baker	2	...	...
9 Wilson, b Baker	1	...	...
11 Smith b Calthorpe	34	...	...
1 Sir A. W. White, b Lagden	14	...	...
10 Dolphin, not out	0	...	...
Extras	20	Extras	...
Total	296	Total	...

Wkts 1 2 3 4 5 6 7 8 9 10 | 1 2 3 4 5 6 7 8 9 10
Runs 24 34 72 101 229 231 235 263 296 296 | ... ...

Umpires—C. E. Richardson and A. Millward.

Play will commence First Day at 12, other two days at 11.30. Luncheon, First Day, 2—2.45; other two days, 1.30—2.15. Stumps drawn at 6.30.

MATCHES TO COME.

June 4, 5, 6.—University v. M.C.C. and Ground.*
June 8, 9, 10.—University v. Free Foresters.*
June 11, 12, 13.—University v. The Army.*

* Free Admission to Ladies will be suspended at these Matches.

D. M. HAYWARD (Custodian), DEALER in all kinds of CRICKET GOODS. BATS from the BEST MAKERS.

MISSES C. & J. SMITH, DRESSMAKERS & COSTUMIERS,
58, DEVONSHIRE ROAD. CAMBRIDGE.

Hy. Smith, Printer, 58, Devonshire Road, Cambridge.

Born at Thames Ditton, Surrey in 1893, the son of Reginald, the former Surrey player (1878-79), Miles Howell (Repton and Oriel, Oxford), was an opening right-handed batsman and outstanding outfielder. Learning his early cricket at Repton School, he later went on to achieve blues at Oxford in 1914 and 1919 when he was captain of the dark blues. Howell later represented Surrey in 36 matches between 1919 and 1925, during which time he scored 1,117 runs (av. 23.76) with a highest score of 99. In 1922 he represented the Combined Universities versus Glamorgan, under the captaincy of W. Osborne. A noted amateur international footballer, he achieved caps against Ireland, Wales, Belgium (as captain) and France between 1919 and 1920, during which time he also represented the Corinthian Casuals. He died in Worplesdon, Surrey in 1976.

Born in Denmark Hill, London in 1894, Arthur Gilligan (Dulwich and Pembroke, Cambridge) was a right-handed, middle order batsman, right-arm fast-medium bowler and good fielder. He represented Cambridge University between 1919 and 1920, attaining blues in both years. Whilst at Fenner's, Gilligan shared in both the eighth and tenth wicket partnership records for Cambridge University: 145 for the eighth wicket with H. Ashton versus Free Foresters at Fenner's in 1920 and 177 for the tenth wicket with J.H. Naumann versus Sussex at Hove in 1919. He played eighteen matches for the light blues, scored 438 runs (av. 23.05) with a top score of 101, bagged 71 wickets (av. 24.69) with a best performance of 6 for 52 and he held 12 catches. He later went on to represent Surrey in three matches in 1919 and Sussex between 1920 and 1932 in 227 matches. He played eleven Tests for England between 1922/23 and 1924/25, touring abroad three times. He played a total of 337 first-class matches during his career, scoring 9,140 runs (av. 20.08). He bagged 868 wickets (av. 23.20) with a best of 8 for 25 and held 180 catches. He died in Pulborough, Sussex in 1976.

Born in Denmark Hill, London in 1893, Frank Gilligan (Dulwich and Worcester, Oxford) was a right-handed middle order batsman and wicketkeeper. He represented Oxford University between 1919 and 1920, achieving blues in both years, and during the 1920 season he captained the side. He later moved to Essex, whom he represented in 79 matches between 1919 and 1929. His final first-class appearance was for MCC in 1935 and he later emigrated to New Zealand to become headmaster at Wanganui Grammar School in Wellington, where he died in 1960.

Born in Hampstead, London in 1901, Greville Stevens (University College School, Brasenose, Oxford), was a right-handed middle order batsman, leg break bowler and good close fielder. He attended University College School and Oxford University, where he attained blues in all four years between 1920 and 1923 and he captained the side in his last year. He then went on to represent Middlesex 127 times between 1919 and 1932, during which time he accumulated 5,434 runs (av. 30.19) with seven centuries, including a highest score of 170 not out. He bagged 385 wickets (av. 27.42) with a best haul of 8 for 38 and he held 107 catches. He hit 1,000 runs in a season twice with a best of 1,434 (av. 33.34) in 1923. In 1919, whilst playing in a house match at school, he hit 466 and immediately afterwards was selected to play for the Gentlemen versus Players at Lord's. He played ten Tests for England between 1922/23 and 1929/30, accumulating 263 runs (av. 15.47) and taking 20 wickets (av. 32.40) with a best of 5 for 90. He toured abroad four times with MCC to South Africa in 1922/23 and 1927/28, to the West Indies in 1929/30 and with Lord Tennyson's XI to Jamaica in 1931/32. His final first-class match was for MCC and H.D.G. Leveson-Gower's XI in 1933. He died in Islington, London in 1970.

Conrad Johnstone (Rugby and Pembroke, Cambridge) was born in Sydenham, London in 1895. Educated at Rugby School and Cambridge University, he attained blues in both years between 1919 and 1920. He later represented Kent in 36 matches between 1919 and 1933. A left-handed opening batsman, he accumulated 1,186 runs (av. 21.96) with a top score of 102 against Gloucestershire at Maidstone in 1925. He also took 8 wickets (av. 25.50) with a best of 3 for 4 with his right-arm medium paced bowling and he held 18 catches. He represented the Europeans from 1926/27 to 1947/48, and Madras between 1934/35 and 1944/45 whilst serving in India. He was awarded the CBE for his services to the game of cricket in Madras, India and he also served Kent CCC as president in 1966, captained Cambridge University at golf in 1920 and he played his final first-class matches whilst in England in 1939 for the Free Foresters. He died at Eastry, near Sandwich, Kent in 1974.

Douglas Jardine (Winchester and New, Oxford) was born in Bombay, India in 1900 while his Scottish father was Advocate-General of Bombay. He learnt his cricket at Winchester before gaining three Oxford blues between 1920 and 1923. Normally sporting the Harlequin Club cap, as seen in the cartoon, he was a forceful right-handed batsman, reliable leg-break bowler and handy fielder. He later represented Surrey from 1921 to 1933 and he played 141 matches for them, scoring 7,037 runs (av. 44.53) with 14 hundreds and a highest innings of 167. He also bagged 25 wickets (av. 36.64) and he held 102 catches. Jardine played twenty-two Tests for England, captained his country on fifteen occasions and led the side to nine victories. He was without doubt the most controversial Test captain in the history of the game, having devised the 'bodyline' tactics in Australia during the 1932/33 series to reduce Don Bradman's prolific run-getting. In Test matches he accumulated 1,296 runs (av. 48.00) with a highest score of 127 against the West Indies at Old Trafford, Manchester in 1933. By profession Jardine was a solicitor and he later wrote four cricket books. He contracted tick fever whilst in Southern Rhodesia and later died at Montreux, Switzerland in 1958.

Raymond Robertson-Glasgow (Charterhouse and Corpus Christi, Oxford) was born in Murrayfield, Edinburgh in 1901. He represented Oxford University between 1920 and 1923, attaining blues in all four years before he headed down to Taunton where he represented Somerset from 1920 to 1935 in 77 matches. His last first-class match was for the Free Foresters in 1937. A right-arm fast medium bowler, he bagged 464 wickets (av. 25.77) with a best haul of 9 for 38 for Somerset versus Middlesex at Lord's in 1924. As a lower order right-handed batsman, he amassed 2,102 runs (av. 13.22) with a top score of 80 and he held 88 catches. After retiring he became one of the most outstanding cricket writers, both as a journalist and as a writer of notable books on the history of the game of cricket. Suffering from depression, he committed suicide in 1965.

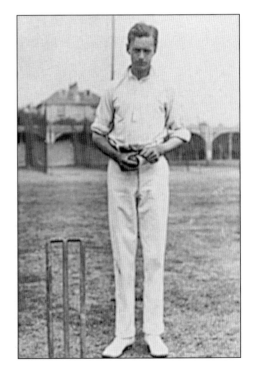

Five

From the 1920s to the 1960s

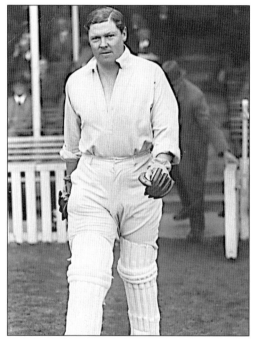

Percy Chapman (Oakham, Uppingham and Pembroke, Cambridge) was an adventurous left-handed batsman and fine gully fielder. He topped the batting average (av. 111.33) at Uppingham School in 1917 and he scored 118 for Cambridge University versus Essex at Fenner's, Cambridge on his first-class debut in 1920, achieving a blue as a freshman. Chapman represented Cambridge University between 1920 and 1922. Between 1922 and 1930 he achieved three hundreds at Lord's: 102 not out versus Oxford University, 160 for Gentlemen versus Players and 121 for England versus Australia. Martin Donnelly for Oxford later equalled this distinction between 1946 and 1949. Prior to joining Kent in 1924, Chapman represented his native Berkshire and played for England whilst still active in Minor County's cricket. He captained England in seventeen of his twenty-six Tests, winning a record first nine games and he regained the Ashes at Kennington Oval in 1926. He scored 925 runs (av. 28.90) with a top score of 121 versus Australia at Lord's in 1930. He held 32 catches and toured abroad three times. A popular man, he captained Kent from 1931 to 1936, making 194 appearances for them and scoring 6,681 runs (av. 26.93) with 8 centuries.

Clement Gibson (Eton and Clare, Cambridge) was born in Entre Rios, Argentina in 1900. He was a right-handed batsman and right-arm medium bowler and represented the light blues from 1920 to 1921, winning blues in both years. He played 18 matches, scored 337 runs (av. 22.46) with a top score of 46 not out, bagged 76 wickets (av. 21.53) with a best haul of 6 for 76 and held 6 catches. He later played 26 matches for Sussex from 1919 to 1926 and Argentina from 1926/27 to 1937/38. He toured abroad with MCC twice in 1922/23 and 1932 and, despite spending much of his life in Argentina, played the last of his 84 first-class matches for MCC in 1939. He died in Buenos Aires, Argentina in 1976.

A highly powerful influence on the game of cricket and a major force at Lord's for over sixty years as a high-class all-rounder, captain, selector and administrator, Sir George 'Gubby' Allen CBE TD (Eton and Trinity, Cambridge) was born at Bellevue Hill, Sydney in 1902. He represented Middlesex in 146 first-class matches from 1921 to 1950 and Cambridge University between 1922 and 1923. Representing his country in twenty-five Tests from 1930 to 1947/48, he toured abroad three times, including the 1932/33 Ashes series, when he refused to adopt 'bodyline' tactics. He scored 750 runs with a top score of 122 versus New Zealand at Lord's in 1931 and he took 81 wickets with a best of 7 for 80 versus India at Kennington Oval in 1936. He was the second-oldest Test captain after W.G. Grace, at forty-five years and 254 days, when he led the MCC tour to the West Indies in 1947/48. He played a total of 265 first-class matches, scoring 9,232 runs and he took 788 wickets. In 1929 at Lord's he achieved 10 for 40 (8 clean bowled) versus Lancashire. President of MCC in 1963-64, the former 'Q' Stand at Lord's was named after him. He was knighted for his services to cricket in 1986 and he died in 1989.

Born in Chelsea, London in 1901, Sir William Hill-Wood (Eton and Trinity, Cambridge) represented Cambridge University in 1922. Hill-Wood played 14 matches for Cambridge, during which time he hit 556 runs (av. 27.80) with a highest score of 81, took 14 wickets (av. 28.85) with a best of 2 for 3 and he held 8 catches. A solid right-handed batsman and leg-break bowler, he later represented Derbyshire in 35 matches from 1919 to 1936 and the last of his 63 first-class matches was for MCC in 1939. He died in Kensington, London in 1980.

Born at Cartagena, Spain in 1903, Henry Enthoven (Harrow and Pembroke, Cambridge), was a right-handed middle order batsman and a right-arm medium pace bowler. He went to school at Harrow and went on to Cambridge University, where he attained blues in all four years between 1923 and 1926. He made his Middlesex debut in 1925 and represented the county 123 times until 1936. He amassed 7,362 runs (av. 27.16) with 9 centuries and a top score of 139. His best season was 1926 when he hit 1,129 runs (av. 31.36). He also took 252 wickets (av. 32.13) with a best performance of 6 for 64 and he held 78 catches. He captained Cambridge University in 1926, and Middlesex jointly with Nigel Haig between 1933 and 1934. He toured with MCC to Canada in 1937 and his final first-class match was for MCC in 1948. He died in Kensington, London in 1975.

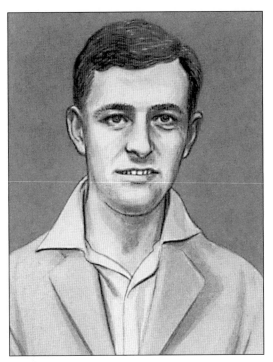

Born in Paddington, London in 1904, Edward Dawson (Eton and Magdalene, Cambridge) represented Cambridge University between 1924 and 1927. He played for Leicestershire from 1922 to 1934 in 174 matches and England between 1927/28 and 1929/30 in five Tests. Dawson played 49 matches for Cambridge whilst scoring 2,581 runs (av. 31.09) with a top score of 140, and he held 18 catches for the light blues. He captained Cambridge in 1927 and Leicestershire in 1928, 1929, 1931 and 1933. He died in Idmiston, Wiltshire in 1979.

Born in Sarodar, India in 1905, K.S. Duleepsinhji (Cheltenham and Clare, Cambridge) represented Cambridge University between 1925 and 1926 and again in 1928, before he represented Sussex and England. Duleepsinhji scored a record 254 not out for Cambridge University versus Middlesex at Fenner's in 1927, which is the highest individual innings in first-class cricket for the light blues. He played 32 matches for Cambridge and scored 2,333 runs (av. 44.01), bagged 15 wickets (av. 33.33) and held 40 catches. He also played 119 matches for Sussex between 1924 and 1932, the Hindus in 1928/29 and twelve Tests for England between 1929 and 1931. He played a total of 205 first-class matches, whilst scoring 15,485 runs (av. 49.95) with a highest score of 333 for Sussex versus Northamptonshire at Hove in 1930, and he held 256 catches. He died in Bombay in 1959 of a heart attack.

Born at Calcutta, India in 1905, Errol Holmes (Malvern and Trinity, Oxford) was a hard-hitting right-handed middle order batsman and right-arm fast-medium bowler. At Oxford University he attained blues in all three years between 1925 and 1927 and he also achieved a blue at soccer as a freshman in 1925. While at University during his season as skipper of the dark blues, he recorded a career best 236 versus the Free Foresters at the University Parks in 1927. Holmes later represented Surrey between 1924 and 1955 in 198 matches, scoring 8,837 runs (av. 34.25) with 15 hundreds and a highest innings of 206 versus Derbyshire at the picturesque Queens Park, Chesterfield in 1935. He also bagged 173 wickets (av. 35.46) with a best performance of 6 for 16 and he held 145 catches, usually at short slip. He achieved 1,000 runs in a season six times and his best season was 1935 when he amassed 1,925 runs (av. 41.84). Playing very little cricket between 1928 and 1933, he returned to captain Surrey from 1934 to 1938, with a second spell at the helm in 1947 and 1948. Holmes represented England in five Tests between 1934/35 and 1935 and he led the MCC team to Australia and New Zealand in 1934/35. He toured abroad on three occasions and he died of a heart attack in Marylebone, London in 1960.

Born in Stafford in 1906, R.W.V. 'Walter' Robins (Highgate and Queen's, Cambridge) was an outstanding right-handed all-rounder. He first appeared for Middlesex in 1925 during his final term at Highgate School before going to Cambridge University, where he achieved a blue in each of his three years between 1926 and 1928. A dynamic captain who made things happen, he led Middlesex in three spells (1935 to 1938, 1946 to 1947 and 1950), winning the championship in 1947. Playing a total of 379 first-class matches he scored 13,884 runs with 11 centuries and he recorded a top score of 140 for Middlesex versus Cambridge University at Fenner's in 1930. He took 969 wickets with a best performance of 8 for 69 for Middlesex versus Gloucestershire at Lord's in 1929 and he held 221 catches. Representing England in nineteen Tests between 1929 and 1937, he captained his country three times in 1937 versus New Zealand and he achieved 612 runs with a top score of 108 versus South Africa at Old Trafford, Manchester in 1935 bagging 64 wickets. He later acted as a Test selector (1946 to 1949, 1954 and 1964). He attained a blue at soccer whilst at Cambridge University and represented Nottingham Forest. He died in Marylebone, London in 1968.

A most gifted all-round athlete, Bryan Valentine (Repton and Pembroke, Cambridge) excelled at lawn tennis whilst studying at Repton School. Later, at Cambridge University, he collected blues at cricket in 1929 and was also a more than useful golfer. He made his debut for Kent in 1927, although he did not secure a regular place in the county side until 1931. In 1933 he scored 1,653 runs (av. 36.73) and consequently was chosen for the MCC tour of India in 1933/34. He hit 134 versus India at Bombay on his Test debut and went on to play seven Tests, scoring 454 runs (av. 64.85) with two centuries. At Oakham in 1938 versus Leicestershire he made his highest score of 242 and in 1938/39 he toured South Africa, scoring 112 at Cape Town. He was awarded the MC during the Second World War and captained Kent from 1946 to 1948. He made 308 appearances for Kent, scoring 14,131 runs (av. 30.52) with 25 centuries and he held 243 catches. He became president of Kent CCC in 1967 and served on the club committee for many years until his death in Otford, Kent in 1983.

Ian Peebles (Glasgow Academy and Brasenose, Oxford), was born in Aberdeen in 1908, where his talent was discovered at the age of thirteen by George Geary, and he then moved south to play for Chiswick Park C.C. in London. Making his first-class debut at nineteen for the Gentlemen versus Players at Kennington Oval in 1927, his first wicket was Andy Sandham. He later represented Middlesex from 1928 to 1948, playing 251 first-class matches; he took 923 wickets with a best performance of 8 for 24 and scored 2,313 runs. He played only one Varsity match for Oxford University in 1930, taking 13 for 237, and also represented Scotland in 1937. Playing thirteen Tests for England between 1927/28 and 1931, he toured abroad twice to South Africa. He took 45 Test wickets with a best performance of 6 for 63 versus South Africa at Johannesburg in 1930/31. Captaining Middlesex in 1939, his career ended tragically following damage to his eye in a wartime air raid. He subsequently entered the wine trade and later became the cricket correspondent of *The Times* and wrote several cricket books. He died at Speen, Buckinghamshire in 1980.

Born in Paddington, London in 1909, Robert Scott (Winchester and Magdalen, Oxford) the brother of P.M.R. (Oxford University) and grandson of C. Marriott (Oxford University), also represented Oxford University in 1930 and 1931. He attained a blue in 1931 before going on to represent Sussex in 66 matches from 1931 to 1934. In total he played 86 first-class matches, scored 2,042 runs (av. 19.82), took 134 wickets (av. 26.82) and held 54 catches. He died in Paddington, London in 1957.

Born at Rondebosch, Cape Town, South Africa in 1909, Harold Owen-Smith (Diocesan College, South Africa and Magdalen, Oxford), was a useful right-handed middle order batsman, slow leg-break bowler and excellent outfielder. Representing his native Western Province between 1927/28 and 1949/50 and Oxford University where he attained blues in all three years between 1931 and 1933, he went on to represent Middlesex between 1935 and 1937. He scored 993 runs (av. 24.83) with a highest score of 77 and he took 100 wickets (av. 21.50) with a best performance of 6 for 68 for Middlesex. During his career he played 101 matches, accumulated 4,059 runs (av. 26.88) with three centuries with a top score of 168 not out, took 319 wickets (av. 23.22) with a best of 7 for 153 and he held 93 catches. Playing five Tests for South Africa, he scored 252 runs (av. 42.00) with a top score of 129 and he held 4 catches. He toured abroad once, to England in 1929, when he scored 1,168 runs (av. 35.89) and took 30 wickets (av. 25.80). A good all-round sportsman, he was awarded blues for boxing and rugby whilst at Oxford and he went on to captain England at the former. He died at Rosebank, Cape Town, South Africa in 1990.

Born in Leytonstone, Essex in 1911, Ken Farnes (Royal Liberty School, Romford and Pembroke, Cambridge) represented Cambridge University between 1931 and 1933 before he played county cricket for Essex in 79 matches from 1930 to 1939 and England in fifteen Tests between 1934 and 1938/39. Farnes played 30 matches for Cambridge, scored 218 runs (av. 6.81), bagged 113 wickets (av. 20.28) with a best haul of 6 for 71 and he held 13 catches. He died in Chipping-Warden, Oxfordshire in 1941.

Born in 1911, Jack Davies (Tonbridge and St. John's, Cambridge) studied at Tonbridge, where he represented the school XI between 1927 and 1930 and was captain of the school during his last year before he went up to Cambridge. He represented Cambridge University between 1933 and 1934 and he later made his Kent debut in 1934. He played 99 matches for Kent until 1951, scoring 4,059 runs (av. 25.36) as a right-handed batsman, with a top score of 168 versus Worcestershire at Worcester in 1946. He took 197 wickets (av. 29.81) with a best haul of 7 for 20 with his slow off-break bowling and he held 55 catches, usually at cover point, where his bald head was most often seen catching opposing batsman. He later went on to act as secretary of Cambridge University Cricket Club at Fenner's and was frequently seen at the ground. He also played rugby for Blackheath and Kent. He later acted as MCC president and died in Cambridge in 1996.

Born in Dereham, Norfolk in 1914, Mike Barton (Winchester and Oriel, Oxford) was a right-handed middle order batsman and good slip fielder. He represented Oxford University from 1935 to 1937, attaining blues in 1936 and 1937. He later moved to Kennington Oval and he played 110 matches for Surrey from 1948 to 1954. He represented his native Norfolk in minor county matches from 1933 to 1947 and he captained Surrey between 1949 and 1951. In total he played 147 first-class matches, scored 5,965 runs (av. 25.82) and he held 117 catches. After retiring from the game he served as president of Surrey in 1983.

Wilfred Wooller (Rydal and Christ's, Cambridge) was born in Rhos-on-Sea in 1912 and represented Cambridge University between 1935 and 1936. He attained blues in both years, playing 18 games for Cambridge. He scored 607 runs (av. 24.28) with a top score of 77, bagged 47 wickets (av. 28.44) with a best of 7 for 20 and he held 7 catches. He later represented Glamorgan as a right-handed batsman, right-arm medium fast bowler and good close fielder in 400 matches between 1938 and 1962. In total he played 430 first-class matches whilst scoring 13,593 runs (av. 22.57) with a top score of 128, bagged 958 wickets (av. 26.96) with a best haul of 8 for 45 and he held 413 catches. He held various positions for Glamorgan CCC from captain (1947 to 1960), and secretary (1947 to 1977) to president (1991-1996) when he died.

BILL
MURRAY-WOOD

Playing his early cricket at Mill Hill and at Oxford University between 1936 and 1938 and attaining a blue in 1936, William Murray-Wood (Mill Hill and Oriel, Oxford), captained Kent in 1952 and 1953. He was born in Dartford in 1917 and was a hard hitting middle order right-handed batsman and useful leg-break bowler who represented Kent in 77 matches from 1936 to 1953. On his first-class debut whilst at Oxford, he scored 106 not out against Gloucestershire at the University Parks in 1936. His best season was when he scored 1,658 runs (av. 13.59) with a top score of 107 for Kent versus Sussex at Tunbridge Wells in 1952, took 47 wickets (av. 40.70) and he held 29 catches. He toured abroad twice with a Combined Universities side to Jamaica in 1938/39 and with Stuart Surridge to Bermuda in 1961. He died in Southwark, London in 1968.

Born in Cheltenham in 1917, Desmond Eagar (Cheltenham and Brasenose, Oxford) represented Oxford University between 1938 and 1939 and he attained a blue in 1939. Eagar represented Gloucestershire in 21 matches between 1935 and 1939 and Hampshire in 311 matches between 1946 and 1957. In total he amassed 12,178 runs (av. 21.86) with a top score of 158 not out, bagged 31 wickets (av. 47.77) and he held 369 catches. He later went on to become secretary of Hampshire and he no doubt influenced his son, Patrick, who has established himself as the leading cricket photographer in the Northern Hemisphere from his studios in Kew, London. He also attained a blue in hockey whilst at Oxford and he died in Kingsbridge, Devon in 1977.

George Mann (Eton and Pembroke, Cambridge) was born in Byfleet, Surrey in 1917 and captained Eton, before representing Cambridge University in 1938 and 1939. A powerful middle order batsman who was particularly strong on the leg-side, he once hit a six straight over the main football stand roof at Headingley, Leeds onto the adjacent rugby field. Playing for Middlesex from 1937 to 1954, he played 166 first-class matches, scoring 6,350 runs with a career best 136 not out for England versus South Africa at Port Elizabeth in 1948/49. Captaining Middlesex in 1948 and 1949, he was unable to lead the 1950/51 MCC tour to Australia due to commitments in his family-owned brewery, but still played seven Tests between 1948 and 1949. The Mann family provided the only example of successive generations skippering England in a single Test. He later acted as TCCB Chairman from 1978 to 1983, following the 'Packer' affair and subsequently became President of MCC in 1984/85.

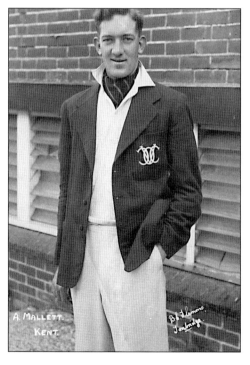

Born in Dulwich, London in 1924 and the father of N.V.H. (Oxford University) Anthony Mallett (Dulwich and Brasenose, Oxford) represented Oxford University from 1947 to 1948 and he won blues in both years. He then played for Kent between 1946 and 1953 in 33 matches and he also toured Canada with MCC in 1951.

New Zealand Test batsman Martin Donnelly (New Plymouth Boys High School, Canterbury University and Worcester, Oxford) represented Oxford University between 1946 and 1947 and captained the side during his final season in 1947. Born in Auckland in 1917, Donnelly was a forceful left-handed top order batsman, slow left-arm bowler and fine fielder. He played a total of 131 first-class matches, scoring 9,250 runs (av. 47.43) during his career which included 43 centuries and a highest innings of 208 not out for MCC versus Yorkshire at Scarborough in 1948. Other than Oxford, he also represented Wellington (1936/37-1940/41), Canterbury (1938/39-1939/40), Middlesex (1946) and Warwickshire (1948-1950). In 1937 he made his Test debut for New Zealand, going on to play seven Tests until 1949, with a top score of 206 versus England at Lord's in 1949. Whilst at Oxford he attained blues for rugby union and also represented England. He died in 1999.

H.A. 'Tony' Pawson (Winchester and Christ Church, Oxford) was the son of A.G. (Worcestershire) and nephew of A.C. (Oxford University). Born in Chertsey in 1921, he was a stylish right-handed batsman, useful off-break bowler and good fielder, playing 43 matches for Kent between 1946 and 1953. Born in 1921, he attained blues in both years whilst at Oxford in 1947 and 1948, captaining the dark blues in his second season. He scored 2,100 runs (av. 33.33) with a top score of 137 for Kent versus Essex at Maidstone in 1950, took 4 wickets (av. 32.75) and held 16 catches. He played football whilst at Oxford, attaining a blue for soccer and he later played professionally for Charlton Athletic like many other Kent cricketers. A highly-respected cricket writer, he was awarded an OBE for services to his second sporting love, fishing. His father, A.G. 'Guy', captained the Oxford side in 1910, having represented the side between 1908 and 1911.

Born in Lahore in 1925, Abdul Harfeez Kardar (Islamia College, Punjab University, and University, Oxford) was an attacking middle order left-handed batsman and slow left-arm bowler. He represented Northern India (1943/44 to 1945/46) and Muslims (1944/45) before playing for Oxford University between 1947 and 1949. He attained blues in all three years and after leaving University he represented Services (1953/54 to 1954/55), and Warwickshire in 50 matches from 1948 to 1950. He played Test cricket for two nations: India in 1946 (three Tests) and Pakistan from 1952/53 to 1957/58 (twenty-three Tests). He captained Pakistan in their first twenty-three Tests in history. In total he played 174 first-class matches, scored 6,832 runs (av. 29.83) with a highest score of 173. He also took 344 wickets (av. 24.55) and he held 110 catches.

Born in Westcliff-on-Sea in 1923, all-rounder Trevor Bailey (Dulwich and St. John's, Cambridge) represented Cambridge University between 1947 and 1948 and he attained blues in both years. He played 22 matches for Cambridge, scoring 861 runs (av. 34.44) with a highest score of 123 not out, bagged 87 wickets (av. 21.25) with a best performance of 5 for 32 and he held 14 catches. He later represented Essex from 1946 to 1967 in 482 matches and England in sixty-one Tests from 1949 to 1958/59. During his career he played 682 first-class matches, scored 28,641 runs (av. 33.42) with a top score of 205 not out for Essex versus Sussex at Eastbourne in 1947, took 2,082 wickets (av. 23.13) with a best haul of 10 for 90 for Essex versus Lancashire at Vista Road, Clacton-on-Sea in 1949 and he held 428 catches. Since retiring he has written several books on the game and has commentated on cricket, both on the television and radio. A talented soccer player, he achieved a blue whilst at Cambridge and he represented Walthamstow in the FA Amateur Cup Final in 1951/52.

CLIVE VAN RYNEVELD

Left: Born in Clapton, London in 1926, Doug Insole CBE (Sir George Monoux, Walthamstow and St. Catherine's, Cambridge) was a right-handed middle order batsman, right-arm medium pace bowler and excellent fielder and occasional wicketkeeper. He represented Cambridge University between 1947 and 1949, attaining blues in all three years, and he captained the University in 1949, his last season at Fenner's before he played regular county cricket. He played for Essex from 1947 to 1963 in 345 matches and he later represented England in nine Tests from 1950 to 1957. Insole played 36 matches whilst at University, scored 1,800 runs (av. 37.50) with a highest innings of 161 not out, took 12 wickets (av. 30.08), held 37 catches and took 5 stumpings. In total he played 489 first-class matches and scored 25,241 runs (av. 37.61) with 54 hundreds and a highest innings of 219 not out for Essex versus Yorkshire at Colchester in 1949. He also took 138 wickets (av. 33.95) with a best haul of 5 for 22, held 366 catches and took 6 stumpings. Since retiring from the game he has served as a Test selector, chairman of the Test and County Cricket Board, chairman of Essex and was awarded the CBE for his services to cricket. A useful soccer player, he won a blue whilst at Cambridge and also represented Southend United and Corinthian Casuals in the FA Amateur Cup Final of 1955/56. *Centre:* Clive van Ryneveld (Diocesan College, South Africa and University, Oxford) was born in Cape Town, South Africa in 1928. A right-handed batsman, leg-break bowler and useful fielder, he represented Oxford University between 1948 and 1950, attaining blues all three years and he captained the side in 1949. He also represented Western Province between 1946/47 and 1962/63 and his native South Africa in nineteen Tests from 1951 to 1957/58. In total he played 101 first-class matches, scored 4,803 runs (av. 30.20), bagged 206 wickets (av. 30.24) and held 71 catches. An excellent rugby footballer, he played at stand off for Oxford University attaining blues, and also played for England. Since his retirement from the game he has been active in the South African government. *Right:* Hubert Doggart (Winchester and King's, Cambridge) was born in Earl's Court, London in 1925. He represented Cambridge University between 1948 and 1950, winning blues in all three years and captaining the University side during the 1950 season. Hubert Doggart scored 215 not out on his University debut versus Lancashire at Fenner's in 1948 and 2,599 runs (av. 55.29) with 7 hundreds. He took 29 wickets (av. 33.82) with a best performance of 3 for 11 and held 29 catches for the light blues. He also represented Sussex in 155 matches from 1948 to 1961 and played two Tests for England in 1950. He attained blues whilst at Cambridge in soccer, squash, rackets and rugby fives. He is currently tireless in his work for the Friends of Arundel Castle CC.

Born at North Latchford, Cheshire in 1926, John Dewes
(Aldenham and St. John's, Cambridge) was a left-handed
opening batsman, right-arm medium pace bowler and
excellent outfielder. At Cambridge he attained blues in all
three years between 1948 and 1950. He represented
Middlesex from 1948 to 1956 on 62 occasions, scoring
8,564 runs (av. 41.77) with 18 centuries and this included a
top score of 212 for Cambridge University versus Sussex at
Hove in 1950. He took 2 wickets (av. 33.50) with a best of 1
for 0 and he held 48 catches. He hit 1,000 runs in a season
three times, with a best of 2,432 runs (av. 59.31) in 1950.
John Dewes shared in both the first and second wicket
partnership records for Cambridge University – 349 for the
first wicket with D.S. Sheppard versus Sussex at Hove in
1950 and 429 unfinished for the second wicket with
G.H.G. Doggart versus Essex at Fenner's in 1949. He
represented England in five Tests between 1948 and
1950/51, scoring 121 runs (av. 12.10) with a top score of
67, and he toured abroad once to Australia and New Zealand
in 1950/51. His appearances for Middlesex were restricted
during the 1950s by his career as a teacher. He made his first-
class debut at Lord's in 1945 for England versus Australia and
his final appearance for L.E.G. Ames' XI in 1957. Also a
good hockey player, he gained blues in 1949 and 1950. His
son, A.R., represented Cambridge University in 1978/79,
attaining a blue in 1978.

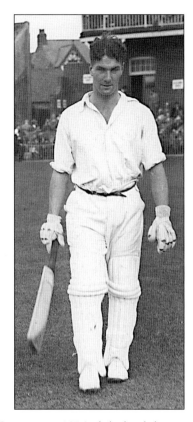

Born in Wiesbaden, Germany in 1926 whilst his father,
J.L., was serving in the Army, Donald Carr OBE (Repton
and Worcester, Oxford) was a middle order right-handed
batsman, slow left-arm bowler and fine close fielder. He
played for Oxford between 1949 and 1951, attained blues
between 1949 and 1951 and was captain in 1950. Carr
represented Derbyshire in 336 matches between 1946
and 1963 (captaining the county from 1955 to 1962) and
he also represented England in two Tests against India in
1951/52. In total he accumulated 19,257 runs (av. 28.61)
with a top score of 170. He also bagged 328 wickets (av.
34.74) with a best haul of 7 for 53 and he held
500 catches. After retiring from first-class cricket, Carr
entered a distinguished career in cricket administration,
initially as secretary of Derbyshire between 1960 and
1962. He later moved to Lord's, where he was assistant
secretary of MCC (1962-1967), secretary of the Test &
County Cricket Board (1973-1986) and secretary of the
Cricket Council (1974-1986). He was manager on three
MCC tours abroad between 1964/65 and 1973/74. Whilst
at Oxford he attained blues at soccer and he represented
Pegasus in the 1950/51 and 1952/53 FA Amateur Cup
Finals at Wembley. Since 1996 he has been the president
of the Hertfordshire Cricket Society and he is the father
of John Carr.

Born at Ealing, Middlesex in 1927, John 'JJ' Warr (Ealing County Grammar School and Emmanuel, Cambridge), was a right-arm fast medium bowler and right-handed tail end batsman. He attained blues in all four years between 1949 and 1952 whilst at Cambridge University and he captained the side in 1951. 'JJ' represented Middlesex 260 times between 1949 and 1960 taking 703 wickets (av. 20.76) with a best performance of 9 for 65 against Kent at Lord's in 1956. He scored 2,744 runs (av. 10.80) with a highest score of 51 and he held 91 catches. Captaining Middlesex between 1958 and 1960, he exceeded 100 wickets in a season twice with a best of 116 (av. 18.17) in 1956. He played two Tests for England with a best of 1 for 76, his only wicket being that of Australian Ian Johnson, caught by Godfrey Evans behind the wicket. He toured abroad five times with MCC to Australia and New Zealand in 1950/51, to Canada in 1951, and to East Africa in 1957/58. He also toured with E.W. Swanton's XI to West Indies in 1955/56 and with the Duke of Norfolk's XI to Jamaica in 1956/57. In 1991 he was elected a trustee of MCC. Retiring from first-class cricket in 1960, he concentrated on a career in the City and is a member of the Jockey Club, a senior steward at Goodwood and a highly respected and witty after-dinner speaker.

Peter May CBE (Charterhouse and Pembroke, Cambridge) was born in Reading in 1929. George Geary of Leicestershire coached him at Charterhouse and he played for Berkshire at minor county level at the age of sixteen. He made his first-class debut for Combined Services before representing Cambridge University between 1950 and 1952. He was awarded blues in 1950, 1951 and 1952 and he was considered the most talented right-handed stroke-making batsman to play in his era. He played 37 matches for Cambridge whilst scoring 2,861 runs (av. 62.19) with a top score of 227 not out. He later represented Surrey from 1950 to 1963, playing 208 first-class matches in total. He scored 14,168 runs (av. 50.41) with 39 hundreds and he held 182 catches. May represented England sixty-six times, captaining them forty-one times, had 21 victories and he toured abroad on seven occasions. In his first Test at Headingley, Leeds in 1951 against South Africa, he scored 138. He accumulated 4,537 Test-runs (av. 46.77). His highest score was 285 not out versus the West Indies at Edgbaston, Birmingham in 1957. Since retiring from the game at only thirty-one, he concentrated on committee work and was an England selector from 1965 to 1968 and again from 1982 to 1988 as chairman of selectors. President-elect of Surrey, he died in 1994.

Robin Marlar (Harrow and Magdalene, Cambridge) was born in Eastbourne, Sussex in 1931. He represented Cambridge University between 1951 and 1953, attaining blues in all three years and he was University skipper in 1953. Marlar played 39 games for Cambridge, scoring 338 runs (av. 11.26), taking 147 wickets (av. 27.89) and holding 21 catches. He also represented Sussex in 223 matches from 1951 to 1968 and he toured the West Indies with E.W. Swanton's XI in 1955/56. Captain of Sussex from 1955 to 1959, he played a total of 289 first-class matches, scored 3,033 runs (av. 9.72), bagged 970 wickets (av. 25.22) with a best haul of 9 for 46 for Sussex versus Lancashire at Hove in 1955 and he held 136 catches. After retiring from the game he became a well-known cricket writer, journalist and commentator. He is presently a committee member of the Sussex County Cricket Club.

Born in Streatham, London in 1932, Raman Subba Row (Whitgift and Trinity Hall, Cambridge) was a sound left-handed top order batsman, slow leg-break and googly bowler and fine slip fielder. He attended Whitgift School prior to making his first-class debut for Cambridge University, where he obtained blues in 1951, 1952 and 1953. In 1953 Raman Subba Row and F.C.M. Alexander shared a fifth wicket partnership record of 220 versus Nottinghamshire at Fenner's. He represented Surrey in 41 matches between 1953 and 1954, scoring 1,663 runs (av. 35.38) with 3 hundreds and a top score of 128, before heading to Northamptonshire where he played 133 matches from 1955 to 1961. His career's best score was 300 for Northamptonshire versus Surrey at Kennington Oval in 1958. With his slow bowling he took his best of 5 for 21 for Cambridge University versus Oxford University in the Varsity match at Lord's in 1951. He achieved 1,000 runs in a season six times, with a best of 1,917 runs (av. 46.75) in 1959. Captaining Northamptonshire from 1958 to 1961, he also played thirteen Tests for England during the same period, scoring 984 runs (av. 46.85) with a highest score of 137 versus Australia at Kennington Oval in 1961. He toured abroad on three occasions, twice as a player and once as a manager to India in 1981/82. He was chairman of Surrey from 1974 to 1978 and was chairman of the Test and County Cricket Board and the Cricket Council between 1985 and 1990. He has recently acted as an ICC referee at Tests around the cricketing globe.

Left: Born in Eureka, California, USA in 1931 and brother-in-law of J.P.K. Asquith (Cambridge University), Dennis Silk OBE (Christ's Hospital and Sidney Sussex, Cambridge) was a right-handed opening batsman and right-arm leg-break bowler who attained blues between 1953 and 1955. He captained the side in 1955 before joining Somerset. Silk represented the light blues 40 times, accumulating 1,824 runs (av. 26.43) with a highest score of 126, and holding 25 catches. He represented Somerset in 33 matches from 1956 to 1960 and he toured abroad four times with MCC from 1957/58 to 1960/61. In all he played 83 first-class matches, scored 3,845 runs (av. 29.80) and he held 45 catches. A notable sportsman, he played rugby football while at Cambridge and for Sussex, and he even appeared for the University at rugby fives. He was awarded the OBE and later served as president of MCC during the 1990s. *Right:* Arthur Walton (Radley and Lincoln, Oxford) was born in Georgetown, Guyana in 1933. He represented Oxford University between 1955 and 1957, attaining blues all three years and he captained the University during the 1957 season before he joined Middlesex. Walton represented Middlesex from 1957 to 1959 in 35 matches and during his career he played 85 first-class matches, scoring 3,797 runs (av. 24.81) with a top score of 152 and he held 47 catches. He also played for Combined Services and Berkshire in minor county matches.

Given the initials 'MCC' by his father, who represented the Europeans versus India in 1926/27, Colin Cowdrey (Tonbridge and Brasenose, Oxford) was coached by Ewart Astill at Tonbridge School and was the youngest player, at thirteen, to play at Lord's. At nineteen he became the youngest player to collect a Kent cap. He attained blues whilst at Oxford between 1952 and 1954 and captained the side in 1954 when the Varsity Match was drawn at Lord's. He represented Kent for twenty-six years and was a prolific right-handed middle order batsman of the highest quality, playing a total of 402 matches and he scored 23,779 runs (av. 42.01) with 58 centuries and a top score of 250 versus Essex at Blackheath in 1959. He was Kent captain between 1957 and 1971 and he held 406 catches and took 27 wickets (av. 47.59) with a best performance of 4 for 22. Cowdrey made his Test debut in 1954/55 versus Australia at Brisbane, playing 114 Tests, scoring 7,624 runs (av. 44.06) with 22 centuries and holding 120 catches. He made 16 tours abroad and his highest score was 182 versus Pakistan at the Oval in 1962. He captained England in 27 Tests with 8 victories. He scored a total of 42,719 runs with 107 centuries and was knighted for his services to cricket in 1992 and named a Lord in 1996. He was president of MCC in 1987/88 and the ICC between 1993 and 1995. Lord Cowdrey died in December 2000.

Left: Born in Leicester in 1933, Mike Smith OBE (Stamford and St. Edmund Hall, Oxford) represented Oxford University between 1954 and 1956, attaining blues in all three years and he captained the side during the 1956 season. He played for Leicestershire in 28 matches from 1951 to 1955, before arriving at Oxford, and after graduating he represented Warwickshire in 430 matches from 1956 to 1975. He also represented England in 50 Tests from 1958 to 1972 and he was one of the most prolific scorers in post-war English cricket history. In total he played 637 first-class matches as a right-handed top order batsman, whilst scoring 39,832 runs (av. 41.84) with 69 centuries and a top score of 204 for Cavaliers versus Natal at Durban in 1960/61. He bagged 121 wickets (av. 41.84) with his right-arm slow medium bowling and took 593 catches as a brilliant short leg fielder. Captain of Warwickshire from 1957 to 1967, he has chaired the cricket and club committees. He led England in 25 Tests, toured abroad nine times and also played rugby football, gaining a blue at fly-half and was also capped by England. He is the father of N.M.K. Smith. *Right:* Born in Milan, Italy in 1935, Ted Dexter (Radley and Jesus, Cambridge) represented Cambridge University between 1956 and 1958, attaining blues in all three years and captaining the side in his last season, 1958. Dexter played 49 matches for Cambridge, scoring 3,298 runs (av. 37.90) with a highest score of 185. He took 50 wickets (av. 27.92) with a best performance of 6 for 69 and he held 35 catches. He also represented Sussex in 137 games between 1957 and 1968, and England in 62 Tests from 1958 to 1968. In total he played 327 first-class matches, amassed 21,150 runs (av. 40.75), bagged 419 wickets (av. 29.92) and held 233 catches. His highest innings of 205 was for England versus Pakistan in Karachi in 1961/62. He was chairman of the England Cricket Committee in 1989 and is also an excellent golfer.

Born in Colombo, Sri Lanka in 1931, leg-break bowler and right-handed batsman Gammi Goonesena (Royal College, Colombo and Queen's, Cambridge) represented Cambridge University between 1954 and 1957, attaining blues in all four years and captaining the side in 1957. Between 1954 and 1957 Gammi Goonesena achieved the most wickets in a career for the University of 208 wickets (av. 21.82) and he also shared in a seventh wicket partnership record of 289 with C.W. Cook versus Oxford University at Lord's during the Varsity Match in 1957. He represented Cambridge in 52 matches and scored 2,309 runs (av. 29.22) with a top score of 211. His best bowling performance was 8 for 39 and he held 24 catches. He also played for Ceylon during the period 1947/48 to 1961/62, Nottinghamshire in 94 games from 1952 to 1964 and New South Wales in 7 matches from 1960/61 to 1963/64. He took 10 for 87 for the Free Foresters in his last first-class match in 1968.

Born in Hall Green, Birmingham in 1936, Alan Smith CBE (King Edward's, Birmingham and Brasenose, Oxford) was a right-handed middle order batsman, occasional right-arm fast medium bowler and wicketkeeper. He represented Oxford University between 1958 and 1960, attaining blues all three years and he captained the side between 1959 and 1960. He also represented Warwickshire in 358 matches from 1958 to 1974 and England in six Tests in 1962/63. In total he amassed 11,027 runs (av. 20.92) with a highest score of 145, took 131 wickets (av. 23.46) and achieved 766 dismissals (715 catches and 61 stumpings) during his illustrious playing career. He served Warwickshire as both captain (1968 to 1974) and secretary (1976-1986). In 1986 he was appointed the Chief Executive of the Test and County Cricket Board (TCCB) until his retirement in 1996 and he also acted as a Test selector during three periods (1969-1973, 1981-1986 and 1989). He won a blue for soccer whilst at Oxford and since retiring from the TCCB has acted as an ICC match referee and was also awarded the CBE.

Tony Lewis (Neath Grammar School and Christ's, Cambridge) was born in Swansea in 1938. A right-handed middle order batsman and leg-break bowler, he represented Cambridge University between 1960 and 1962, attaining blues in all three years. He captained the side in 1962 before going on to represent Glamorgan and England. While at Fenner's, Lewis played 44 games for Cambridge, during which time he scored 3,167 runs (av. 42.22) with a highest score of 148, and he held 20 catches. He played for Glamorgan from 1955 to 1974 in 315 matches and he represented England in nine Tests between 1972/73 and 1973, captaining MCC to India, Pakistan and Sri Lanka in 1972/73. A distinguished career for Cambridge (which included a blue at rugby), Glamorgan and England saw him play 409 first-class matches, whilst accumulating 20,495 runs (av. 32.42), with only 6 wickets and holding 193 catches. After retiring he has served Glamorgan as chairman since 1988, acted as a television commentator and he is currently president of MCC and has strong links with the Welsh Tourist Board.

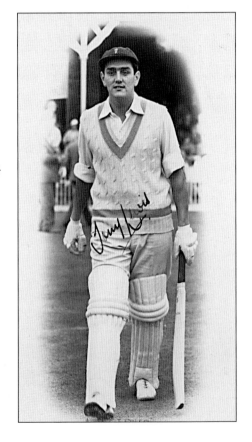

Left: Born in Harrow in 1942, Mike Brearley OBE (City of London and St. John's, Cambridge) was an excellent tactical captain and an outstanding leader of players, who made his first-class debut for Cambridge University in 1961 and represented them until 1964. He later acted as captain in 1963 and 1964. Mike Brearley achieved the highest number of runs in a career for Cambridge University (4,310 runs, av. 38.48) between 1961 and 1964. He represented Middlesex from 1961 to 1983 (1971 to 1982 as captain), as an opening batsman and specialist slip fielder, leading the county to the championship three times. Playing 455 first-class matches, he amassed 25,185 runs with 45 centuries and with a top score of 312 not out for the MCC Under-25 tour versus North Zone at Peshawar in 1966/67, he held 418 catches. He represented England in thirty-nine Tests, with 18 victories in thirty-one Tests as skipper, scoring 1,442 runs with a top score of 91 versus India at Bombay in 1976/77. He toured abroad ten times and he was only the second captain after Len Hutton to regain and successfully defend the Ashes and was the first to lead England to five wins in an Ashes series. Since retiring he has concentrated on psychotherapy, cricket writing and teaching. *Centre:* Born in East Melbourne, Australia in 1938, Colin Drybrough (Highgate and Worcester, Oxford) represented Oxford University between 1960 and 1962 and whilst playing his early cricket at the University Parks he captained the side in 1961 and 1962. He later joined Middlesex and made 92 appearances for them between 1958 and 1964. He captained the county in 1964 and his final first-class match was for MCC in 1967. Whilst at Oxford, Drybrough also attained a blue for soccer. *Right:* The Nawab of Pataudi junior (Winchester and Balliol, Oxford) was born in Bhopal, India in 1941. He represented Oxford University in 1960 and 1963. He was named captain for the 1961 season, although he never played for the University during that season. He also represented Sussex between 1957 and 1970 in 88 matches, Delhi (1960/61 to 1964/65) and Hyderabad (1965/66 to 1975/76). He represented India in forty-six Tests (forty as captain) from 1961/62 to 1974/75. In 1961 he suffered a serious road accident, which damaged his eyesight and meant that he missed the 1961 Varsity match as captain. In total he played 310 first-class matches, accumulating 15,425 runs (av. 33.67) with a highest score of 203 not out for India versus England at Delhi in 1963/64. He also took 10 wickets (av. 77.60) and he held 208 catches.

Left: Born in Port-of-Spain, Trinidad in 1943. Deryck Murray (Queen's Royal, Trinidad and Jesus, Cambridge) was a right-handed middle order batsman, wicketkeeper and occasional off-break bowler. He represented Cambridge University between 1965 and 1966, attaining a blue both years, and he captained the side during the 1966 season. Murray played 24 matches for Cambridge, scoring 1,248 runs (av. 29.02) with a top score of 133. He also took 33 catches and 5 stumpings and, as an occasional spinner, took 1 for 46 with the ball. He represented Trinidad from 1960/61 to 1980/81, Nottinghamshire from 1966 to 1969 in 97 matches and Warwickshire from 1972 to 1975 in 58 matches. He played sixty-two Tests for West Indies from 1963 to 1980 and his career behind the timbers for the West Indies meant that he kept wicket to the likes of Roberts, Holding, Croft, Daniel and Marshall. In total he played 367 first-class matches, scored 13,291 runs (av. 28.33) with a highest score of 166 not out and he achieved 848 dismissals (740 catches and 108 stumpings). Whilst at Cambridge he attained a blue for soccer. Since retiring he has commentated on television for Sky and has captained Vic Lewis' celebrity XI in the annual match against the Royal Household Cricket Club at Windsor Castle. *Centre:* David Acfield (Brentwood and Christ's, Cambridge) represented Cambridge University between 1967 and 1968, and he took 92 wickets (av. 33.39) with a best haul of 6 for 28 whilst at Fenner's. He also scored 358 runs (av. 8.95) with a highest score of 42 and he held 16 catches. An accomplished spinner, he went on to play for Essex and represented them between 1966 and 1986. He played 420 first-class matches, bagging 950 wickets (av. 28.21) with a best performance of 8 for 55. A late order batsman, he scored 1,677 runs (av. 8.18) and held 137 catches. During his sporting career he also fenced for England. *Right:* Born at Streatham, London in 1946, Roger Knight (Dulwich and St. Catherine's, Cambridge) was a left-handed middle order batsman and right-arm medium pace bowler. He represented Cambridge University from 1967 to 1970, achieving blues in all four years. He represented the light blues 48 times, scoring 2,428 runs (av. 28.56) with a highest score of 164 not out, bagged 60 wickets (av. 34.73) with a best haul of 6 for 65 and he held 27 catches. He joined Surrey in 1968 and he represented them in 174 matches, captaining the county from 1978 to 1983, until his retirement in 1984. He left Surrey in 1971 after just three seasons, joining Gloucestershire, for whom he played 105 games until 1975, after which he played for Sussex in 43 matches from 1976 to 1977 before returning to Surrey as skipper. In total he played 387 first-class matches, accumulated 19,558 runs (av. 32.00) with 31 hundreds and a top score of 165 not out. He also took 369 wickets (av. 36.13) with a best performance of 6 for 44 and he held 295 catches. He hit 1,000 runs in a season thirteen times, with a best of 1,350 runs (av. 38.57) in 1989. After a period as headmaster at Worksop College, he was appointed secretary of MCC at Lord's Cricket Ground in 1994.

Six

Oxbridge 1970s to the 1990s

View of the pavilion at Fenner's University Cricket Ground, painted by Kay Chadwick in 1971.

Born in India in 1946, Majid Jahangir Khan (Aitchison College Lahore, Punjab University and Emmanuel, Cambridge) represented Cambridge University between 1970 and 1972. He captained the University side between 1971 and 1972 and Glamorgan between 1973 and 1976. Majid played 29 matches for Cambridge as an opening batsman. He accumulated 2,545 runs (av. 53.02) with a highest score of 200, took 30 wickets (av. 33.66) with a best of 3 for 33 and he held 32 catches. He later represented Glamorgan from 1968 to 1976 in 154 matches, Punjab, Pakistan International Airlines, Queensland, Rawalpindi and Pakistan, in sixty-three Tests from 1964/65 to 1982/83. He played 410 first-class matches during his career, which saw him accumulate 27,444 runs (av. 43.01) with a top score of 241, take 223 wickets (av. 32.14) and 410 catches. Since retiring he has served the Board for Cricket Control in Pakistan as chief executive.

Born in Lusaka, North Rhodesia in 1951, Phillippe 'Phil' Edmonds (Gilbert Rennie High School, Lusaka, Cranbrook and Fitzwilliam, Cambridge), made his first-class debut for Middlesex in 1971 after taking 9 wickets versus Leicestershire at Fenner's in only his second first-class match for Cambridge University. He led Cambridge in his final year in 1973 before taking his slow left-arm skills to Lord's where he represented Middlesex until 1987, although he did return for a single match in 1992. He played a total of 391 first-class matches, scoring 7,651 runs with a top score of 142 for Middlesex versus Glamorgan at Swansea in 1984. He took 1,246 wickets with a best of 8 for 53 versus Hampshire at Bournemouth in 1984 and he held 345 catches. For England he played in fifty-one Tests, between 1975 and 1987. Touring abroad five times, he took 125 wickets with a best of 7 for 66 versus Pakistan at Karachi in 1977/78 and he scored 875 runs. His wife Frances wrote accounts of his last two tours. Now engaged in business, he also writes and commentates on the game and is the chairman of Middlesex CCC's general committee.

Born in Hartford, Cheshire in 1953, the younger son of Lord Rochester, the Hon. Tim Lamb (Shrewsbury and Queen's, Oxford) was schooled at Shrewsbury before going up to Oxford University. He made his first-class debut in 1973 and he attained blues in both years in 1973 and 1974. He represented Middlesex in 36 matches between 1974 and 1977, before moving to Northamptonshire for whom he played 108 matches between 1978 and 1983. During his career with the ball, he took 361 wickets (av. 28.97) with a best performance of 7 for 56 for Northamptonshire versus Cambridge University at Fenner's in 1980. With the bat he scored 1,274 runs (av. 12.49) with a top score of 77 for Middlesex versus Nottinghamshire at Lord's in 1976 and he also held 40 catches. He moved back to Lord's in 1983, when he was appointed secretary/general manager of Middlesex, a post he held until 1987, when he moved to the position of cricket secretary of the Test and County Cricket Board (TCCB). In 1996, after the retirement of Alan Smith, he was appointed Chief Executive of the TCCB and subsequently the England and Wales Cricket Board (ECB) which is now housed in new offices at the Nursery End of the ground at Lord's.

Born in Lahore, Pakistan in 1952, Imran Khan (Aitchison College, Lahore, Worcester Royal Grammar School, Keble, Oxford) is the cousin of Majid Khan, Javed Zaman (Lahore), Humayun Zaman (Lahore), Javed Burki (Pakistan) and nephew of Baqa Jilani (India) and Jahangir Khan (Cambridge University and India). He was a high-class right-handed all-rounder who was a middle order batsman and fast bowler. He represented Oxford University between 1973 and 1975 and captained the University dark blues in 1974. He represented Lahore (1969/70 to 1970/71) before arriving in England. He then went on to represent Worcestershire in 42 matches (1971-1976), Sussex in 131 matches (1977-1988), Dawood Club (1975/76) and New South Wales (1984/85). He represented his native Pakistan in eighty-eight Tests, having made his Test debut in 1971 against England and he played his last match in 1991/92. In all he made 382 first-class appearances, scoring 17,771 runs (av. 36.79) with 30 centuries and a highest innings of 170. He took 1,287 wickets (av. 22.32) with a best performance of 8 for 34 and he held 117 catches.

Making his Kent debut in 1974, Chris Tavaré (Sevenoaks and St. John's, Oxford) played 259 matches for Kent, scoring 14,201 runs (av. 37.97) including 29 centuries and he held 269 catches before departing to Somerset in 1989. He was educated at Sevenoaks School and Oxford University, where he gained a degree in Zoology and blues from 1975 to 1977. He made his first century, 124, for Kent versus Nottinghamshire at Canterbury in 1977. A right-handed number three batsman, he played the anchor-role and was a stylish stroke-maker. He made his Test debut versus West Indies in 1980, when he scored 82 not out at Headingley, Leeds. In 1981 he scored the slowest 50 in England in a Test match and also the quickest 100 off only 27 balls in the Lambert & Butler floodlit match at Crystal Palace FC. He made thirty-one Test appearances for England, scoring 1,753 runs (av. 33.07), including a top score of 149 versus India at Delhi in 1981/82. He captained Kent from 1984 to 1988, when he led them to two cup final defeats at Lord's. He scored 1,430 runs (av. 42.05) in his last season when he helped Kent to within a single point of the County Championship. He went on to captain Somerset during his later career.

Born in Middle Chinnock, Somerset in 1955. Vic Marks (Blundell's and St. John's, Oxford) played his early cricket whilst at Blundell's School, before representing Oxford University between 1975 and 1978. He captained the dark blues between 1976 and 1977. He later joined Somerset representing the Wyverns in 275 matches between 1975 and 1989 . During his career, right-handed Marks played 342 first-class matches, whilst scoring 12,419 runs (av. 30.29) with 5 hundreds and a highest innings of 134. As a useful off-break bowler he bagged 859 wickets (av. 33.28) with a best haul of 8 for 17 and he held 144 catches. He also played six Tests for England from 1982 to 1983/84, scoring 249 runs (av. 27.66) with the bat and 11 wickets (av. 44.00) with the ball. Since retiring from the game, he has been a cricket correspondent, writer and radio commentator on the game.

Paul Parker (Collyer's Grammar School and St. Catherine's, Cambridge) was born in Bulawayo, Zimbabwe in 1956. He represented Cambridge University between 1976 and 1978, attaining blues in all three years before he represented Sussex, Durham and England. Parker played 25 matches whilst at Fenner's. He scored 1,389 runs (av. 34.72) with a best of 215 versus Essex at Fenner's in 1976. He took a best of 2 for 23 with the ball and held 15 catches. Parker represented Sussex from 1976 to 1991 in 289 games, Natal in 1980/81, Durham in 1992 in 20 matches and England in a single Test in 1981. In total he played 352 first-class matches, accumulated 18,495 runs (av. 35.36) and held 244 catches. Whilst at Cambridge he also played rugby football but did not attain a blue.

Nigel Popplewell (Radley and Selwyn, Cambridge), the son of Justice Popplewell, who represented Cambridge between 1949 and 1951, was born in Chislehurst, Kent in 1957. He represented Cambridge University between 1977 and 1979, during which time he played 25 matches, and scored 476 runs (av. 19.83) with a top score of 92. He took 25 wickets (av. 54.08) with a best of 3 for 18 and he held 6 catches, before he joined Somerset in 1979. Popplewell played 118 matches for Somerset until 1985, toured Bangladesh with MCC in 1976/77 and played for Buckinghamshire from 1975 to 1978 in minor county matches. In total he played 143 first-class matches, scored 5,070 runs (av. 27.11) with a highest score of 172, bagged 103 wickets (av. 43.11) and he held 110 catches.

Born in Queenstown, South Africa in 1955, Ian Greig (Queen's College, South Africa and Downing, Cambridge) the younger brother of A.W. 'Tony', represented Cambridge University between 1977 and 1979 and captained the side during the 1979 season. He then went on to represent Border 1974/75 to 1979/80, Griqualand West 1975/76, Sussex in 107 matches from 1980 to 1985 and Surrey in 115 matches from 1987 to 1991. He also represented England in two Tests in 1982. Greig played 22 games for the light blues, during which time he accumulated 669 runs (av. 23.89) with a top score of 96, bagged 32 wickets (av. 38.90) with a best of 4 for 76 and he held 11 catches. He attained a blue for rugby whilst at Cambridge and during his time as captain of Surrey scored 291 against Lancashire at Kennington Oval in 1990, his career best score in 253 first-class matches.

Born in Nairobi, Kenya in 1958, Derek Pringle (Felsted and Fitzwilliam, Cambridge) was a middle order right-handed batsman, and right-arm medium-pace bowler. He represented Felsted School and then went on to represent Cambridge University between 1979 and 1982 and he captained the light blues in 1982. He later represented Essex in 199 matches from 1978 to 1992 and he played thirty Tests for England from 1982 to 1992. Due to being selected to represent England in a Test match during the summer of 1982, he did not play in the Varsity Match at Lord's and so only attained blues in 1979, 1980 and 1981. In total Pringle played 281 first-class matches, scored 8,633 runs (av. 27.93) with a top score of 128, bagged 732 wickets (av. 26.21) with a best performance of 7 for 18 and he held 142 catches. Since retiring he has concentrated on a career as a cricket journalist and he has been a regular contributor to the *Daily Telegraph* newspaper.

Born in Hatton, Ceylon in 1959, Robin Boyd-Moss (Bedford and Magdalene, Cambridge) was a middle order right-handed batsman and slow left-arm bowler. He represented Cambridge University between 1980 and 1983, attaining blues in all four years prior to joining Northamptonshire. Boyd-Moss scored a record 489 runs in a career in Varsity Matches between 1980 and 1983, when he held the distinction of scoring two hundreds in three successive seasons. In total he played 37 matches for Cambridge, scoring 2,090 runs (av. 33.17) with a top score of 139. He also took 25 wickets (av. 35.84) with a best of 5 for 27 and he held 13 catches. He represented Northamptonshire from 1980 to 1987 in 115 games and also played rugby football for Cambridge University and Bedfordshire.

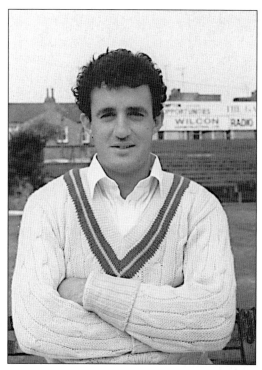

Born at St. John's Wood, London in 1963, son of D.B. (Derbyshire and Oxford University), grandson of J.L. (Army), John Carr (Repton and Worcester, Oxford) was a right-handed opening batsman, off break bowler and useful fielder. He attained blues in all three years between 1983 and 1985 whilst at Oxford University. He represented Middlesex in 191 matches between 1983 and 1996. He accumulated 9,846 runs (av. 39.22) with 20 centuries including a highest score of 261 not out for Middlesex versus Gloucestershire at Lord's in 1995, including 43 fours. He took 33 wickets (av. 35.03) with a best performance of 6 for 61, and he held 243 catches. He hit 1,000 runs in a season five times, with his best season being 1994 when he achieved 1,543 runs (av. 90.76) including six centuries and seven fifties. He played minor county cricket for Hertfordshire in two spells between 1982 and 1984 and again between 1990 and 1991. In 1997 he was appointed the Cricket Operations Manager of the England and Wales Cricket Board (ECB) based at Lord's.

Born in Manchester in 1968, right-handed opening batsman and leg-break bowler Michael Atherton (Manchester Grammar School and Downing, Cambridge) represented Cambridge University between 1987 and 1988 and attained a blue in all three years, captaining the side in 1988 and 1989. Atherton played 25 matches for Cambridge, scoring 1,493 runs (av. 41.47) with a highest innings of 151 not out. He took 36 wickets (av. 46.16) with a best performance of 3 for 58 and he held 22 catches. He has since represented Lancashire and England and has captained his country in Tests and one day internationals. He made his one hundreth Test appearance for England against the West Indies at Old Trafford, Manchester in 2000.

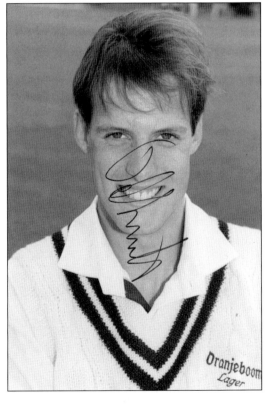

Ed Smith (Tonbridge and Clare, Cambridge) was educated at Tonbridge School and Cambridge University, where he attained blues between 1996 and 1997. He made his Kent debut in 1996 against Derbyshire at Derby aged twenty-one and his best batting performance to-date was 190 for Cambridge University versus Leicestershire at Fenner's, Cambridge in 1997. He has also represented England Under-19 versus New Zealand Under 19 in 1996 and was unlucky not to figure on one of England's 1999/2000 winter tours.